WRITING IN ELEMENTARY SCHOOL SOCIAL STUDIES

Edited by
Barry K. Beyer and Robert Gilstrap

Social Science Education Consortium, Inc.

ERIC Clearinghouse for Social Studies/Social Science Education

Boulder, Colorado

1982

ORDERING INFORMATION

This publication is available from:

Social Science Education Consortium, Inc.
855 Broadway
Boulder, Colorado 80302

ISBN 0-89994-267-9

Price: $10.95

This publication was prepared with funding from the National Institute of Education, U.S. Department of Education, under contract no. 400-78-0006. The opinions expressed do not necessarily reflect the positions or policies of NIE or ED.

CONTENTS

Figures

PREFACE

Johnny may be able to read, but can he write?

Not as well as his counterparts could ten years ago, according to the National Assessment of Educational Progress. The results of NAEP's 1979-1980 National Assessment of Reading and Literature showed that the ability of 17-year-olds to analyze, interpret, and express their views about written prose had declined by approximately 20 percent since 1971. Only 41 percent of the students tested in 1980 were able to compose reasoned, thoughtful answers.

In their report of the study, Reading, Thinking, and Writing (available from NAEP, Suite 700, 1860 Lincoln St., Denver, CO 80295), the NAEP researchers recommended that the curriculum be restructured so as to provide more opportunities for students to develop and practice analytical skills. Testing programs, they suggest, should rely more heavily on essay questions. Teachers in all subject areas should incorporate writing into their programs on a regular basis, and students should have many opportunities to write at length for a variety of purposes. Since using writing activities is time consuming for teachers, administrators should provide institutional support in the form of released time, teaching aides, or smaller classes.

Obviously, if such an approach is to be effective, it must be instituted long before Johnny is 17. Indeed, innovative teachers have effectively used writing activities with children as young as 4 or 5. Students who enter high school without a solid basis in writing are seriously handicapped. Writing must begin in the elementary school--as early as possible, and as often as possible.

However, as the editors of this volume point out, few elementary school teachers have had explicit instruction in using writing with young children, nor do many new teachers or teachers-in-training have much opportunity to observe the effective use of writing in the elementary grades. Teachers may also be handicapped by the scarcity of models for incorporating writing into subject areas other than language arts.

This book is designed to provide elementary school teachers with information, suggestions, and models for using writing in the social studies, from early primary to middle grades. We hope that it will be a useful resource for teachers who are aware of the importance of writing in thinking, learning, and living.

James E. Davis

Associate Director
Social Science Education Consortium, Inc.
ERIC Clearinghouse for Social Studies/
Social Science Education

ACKNOWLEDGMENTS

We wish to thank all those who helped to make this publication a reality. Thanks especially go to all those teachers who so willingly contributed to this professional undertaking by responding to our invitations to prepare manuscripts. We also appreciate very much the aid of our reviewers, Gwen Harrison, Nellie Quander, Jay Weisman, and Dolores Windt. Thanks, too, go to Dale Van Dyke and Patti Summers for helping us to prepare the manuscript for publication and to Ann Williams for her editorial contributions. Finally, we wish to express our sincere appreciation to Sue Woodfine, who typed most of the manuscript--without her patient and diligent work these pages surely would not yet exist!

Barry K. Beyer
Robert Gilstrap

Fairfax, Virginia
October 1981

PROLOGUE

We know more about writing than most elementary school classroom practice usually reveals. Research over the past decade has given us considerable insight into how young children compose as well as knowledge about a variety of instructional techniques that help them improve the ways they compose. Yet, for the most part, the results of this research have not filtered through to classroom teachers, curriculum builders, or textbook authors. Because of this unfortunate communication gap, writing is probably the most misunderstood, misused, and undervalued instructional tool and learning goal in our schools today.

This volume addresses that situation. It speaks specifically to elementary school social studies teachers, supervisors, and administrators as well as to elementary school teacher educators, especially those who share an interest in improving student competence in writing and learning in social studies. We seek one major goal--to introduce instruction in writing into social studies, for the mutual improvement of both. We have chosen to do this essentially by focusing in some depth on a variety of practical, classroom-tested techniques which integrate writing and social studies in the elementary grades.

Why should elementary school educators be concerned about writing in social studies? At least four reasons come readily to mind.

First, although writing is often considered to be a valid instructional goal in elementary school, it is rarely viewed as the learning tool that it is--or could be. In reality, we learn as we write. We invent ideas, we see relationships, and we learn information as we try to describe, explain, illustrate, or justify something to someone in writing. Social studies teachers can use writing as a tool for helping students learn social studies information and concepts.

Second, writing skills, quite properly introduced in language-arts units, must be used across a variety of curriculum areas in order to be mastered by children. Writing is not something we learn how to do once and for all, nor are the skills which constitute writing easily transferred to new contexts from the context in which they are introduced. The way we write is shaped very much by the context in which we write.

Our abilities to write grow and develop as the content and concepts we use become increasingly complex and sophisticated and as our purposes change from entertaining to informing to persuading. By providing instructive opportunities to write in elementary social studies, we can help students refine, extend, and further develop the writing skills introduced elsewhere, and we can also introduce new aspects of writing which are particularly well suited to communicating about social subjects and ideas.

Third, writing is a social act--it is a purposeful interaction between someone with something to say and someone to whom that information is being related. Social studies thus serves as a most useful arena in which to develop and use writing, for its prime function is to develop the skills of and knowledge about social interaction. In social studies youngsters can use writing to better understand themselves as well as to refine these skills and knowledge. They can write to develop a sense of community as well as to participate in that community. They can write to develop, express, and reflect on information and ideas related to social studies subjects and topics. Practicing writing with supervision and continued instruction in social studies offers an opportunity to extend social skills and knowledge as well as improve writing ability in meaningful and purposeful ways.

Finally, writing is actually thinking in action. It involves relationship-making and relationship-sensing as youngsters seek to connect bits of information in order to form or support ideas they infer from this information. Writing also involves a host of other cognitive skills, including those of classifying, analyzing, and evaluating. Writing can thus serve as a useful tool for teaching students various thinking skills--skills that are a time-honored objective of our elementary school curricula.

The remaining chapters in this book attempt to articulate this rationale. They should be read, however, with several caveats in mind.

First, we have elected to emphasize the writing process and its component skills. Throughout these pages we refer to the writing process and to the various stages of this process which should be familiar to elementary educators. Specialists in writing generally divide the writing process into three major phases. These phases, or stages, are usually known as (1) prewriting, (2) writing (or composing), and (3) rewriting (or revising). Each stage is a part of the overall process by which a writer creates and produces a piece of writing. Although each person's writing process is unique and varies with both the writer and the writing task, most children generally move through these three stages when they write.

We believe that children need to be introduced to the writing process by classroom teachers through direct instruction. The resulting awareness of the process can help young writers to organize their thinking and communicate their ideas more clearly to others. Children will then be able to use their understanding of the process when they write independently of the teacher.

Prewriting activities are designed to help children generate, expand, and focus ideas developed from their own background experiences or from such stimuli as objects, books, trips, animals, and resource people. These activities also help children to understand the purpose of writing and to identify an audience. When students are working independently, prewriting activities might include collecting information through reading, interviewing, observing, and remembering as well as experimenting with titles and opening paragraphs and making lists of major ideas.

During the composing stage, it is important that children should be given sufficient time to put their ideas into written form and opportunities to seek help if they need it. A child's first draft, sometimes called a discovery draft, should be written without concern for missing words and mistakes in punctuation and spelling. Correcting these mistakes, revising sentence structure, and paying attention to legible handwriting are done during the rewriting stage. Whether students are working independently or under the direction of the teacher, the emphasis during the composing stage should be on capturing in writing what the writer knows or wants to say about the topic.

Rewriting activities should provide children with opportunities to clarify, refine, and revise ideas; proofread; have conferences with the teacher, a partner, or a small group; and prepare their writing for sharing. When they are working independently, children will develop their writing more fully and try to anticipate all the reader's questions, with attention given to purpose and audience.

Sharing writing is an essential step in the writing process for children, although some writing specialists do not include it as a separate stage. When children share their writings in a classroom setting, one of the teacher's primary responsibilities is to provide an accepting atmosphere in which positive sharing will occur. During the sharing process, children may read their writings to others, publish their writings in school newspapers or book form, display their work, and present their work through other creative ways such as dramatizations and on video or audio tape.

Depending on the purpose, message, and content of the work, a writer may go through other operations not listed in this description of the writing process. This description is a general one, presented to clarify our use of the term throughout this volume. It is also important to point out that, although all writers move through each stage of this process, a child may move back to an earlier stage before moving on to the next; the process is recursive rather than linear.

Second, we do not intend the techniques presented here to be considered either prescriptive or exhaustive. Because of space limitations and the embryonic state of the art of writing instruction, we cannot hope to include explicit mention of all the techniques that specialists recommend in teaching writing. Instead, we have chosen to present a limited number of techniques in enough detail so that they can be replicated in any classroom. However, it is important to remember that many techniques other than those presented here exist to achieve the goal we seek.

Third, these techniques do not stand alone. They are not presented simply as a grab bag of classroom gimmicks. Rather, the teaching techniques described here exist in a curricular context and are supported by considerable research and theory. Thus, we have tried to support these techniques with relevant information about research and theory and with discussion of the curricular and teaching context in which they can be developed and used. Knowledge of some techniques that exist and ability to use them are important tools in improving writing in elementary school social studies. However, only by knowing how these techniques can fit into school curricula, as well as into daily or unit lessons, and why they should be used in certain ways can we bring about meaningful improvement in classroom teaching and in student learning as well.

Finally, this book does not deal with all aspects of the writing process or all the important aspects of writing instruction. We have sacrificed coverage of many topics for in-depth focus on a few. Because our goal is to make classroom writing really possible, we have elected to go into practical detail about two of the most crucial aspects of writing. For students, this crucial factor is getting started. For teachers, the critical function is integrating student writing with social studies. Obviously, much more could be included here even about these two topics; this book is simply a start. Use of the ideas here can actually get writing under way in an elementary social studies classroom. However, for anyone who is seriously interested in a complete writing program, further experimentation and study will be necessary.

Our contributors are strangers neither to elementary education nor to social studies teaching. Although as a group they represent the entire range of educators concerned with writing in elementary social studies--including educational researchers, teacher educators, principals, and curriculum specialists--the majority of authors represented here are classroom teachers. Most of the authors of the articles in Parts II and III teach in elementary school classrooms and actually use the techniques they describe. For many of them, this book represents a first attempt at professional writing for publication. Their styles vary. However, what unites them is that not only are they describing classroom-tested social studies writing techniques, they are also practicing what they are teaching--writing. We are pleased to make their articles the core of this book, for we believe that they are making an important contribution to their own professional development as well as to the potential development of those who will read this book.

These essays are unique. They reveal as much about elementary school teachers and about teaching in general as they do about writing and about social studies in the elementary school classroom. Some relate highly personal experiences, dealing only implicitly with writing or social studies; guidelines for teaching writing must be inferred by the reader. Other articles explain in some detail general writing techniques, often couched in terms of exciting classroom lessons. Still other articles describe in great detail--almost prescriptively--very specific techniques for writing in elementary school social studies.

Most of these articles have several characteristics in common. First, they indicate that writing does not stand as an end in itself in the elementary school social studies classroom. It is, rather, part of a sequence of activities designed to accomplish goals that may range from social participation to knowledge development, learning, skill development, or attitude development--all common social studies goals. Second, these articles acknowledge the importance of prewriting activities as a key to effective student writing. Third, they reflect a commitment to using writing as a tool of social education--as a device for developing social awareness and social interaction skills, for writing itself is an act of social intercourse. Finally, these articles speak directly, almost personally, to the reader; the resulting sense of intimacy--we hope--communicates the enthusiasm the authors have for teaching writing in elementary school social studies.

Now, to reaffirm our purposes, a few final thoughts:

Unfortunately, studying the techniques and ideas presented here will not make one ipso facto an expert in teaching writing in elementary school social studies. However, the study, discussion, classroom use, and adaptation of these ideas can improve both teaching and student learning. This is the goal of this book and of its sponsors.

In addition, we hope that these articles will underscore the point that, although language arts is a significant part of the elementary school curriculum, writing skills taught in that subject area must be used in other curriculum fields if they are to have practical value to children. One learns to write in order to be able to write about something, and social studies provides the perfect area of the curriculum for using this important skill of communication.

We also hope that these articles will provide a clearer idea of the importance of attending to the process of writing as well as to the final product. Although we are only beginning to comprehend the complexity of this process, we do understand some ways in which the process and thus the quality of its products can be enhanced through techniques like those described here.

Finally, we hope that these articles clarify ways to use writing as a tool for helping children learn to think more clearly. For both children and teachers, writing can be a valuable tool for learning, and writing in social studies can be a means to this end as well as an end in itself.

WHAT CHILDREN ARE TELLING US ABOUT WRITING

1. Let me begin writing early because I have something to say that's important to me.

2. Give me time to get started because writing can't be rushed.

3. Let me write about what I know and about what I want to know.

4. Let me write for many audiences.

5. Let me write for many purposes and in many forms.

6. Let me talk with you and others about my writing.

7. Let me revise before editing.

8. Let me publish what I write.

9. Respect what I have to say in my writing.

10. Write with me.

I. RESEARCH ON THE TEACHING OF WRITING

As noted in the prologue, educators know more about how youngsters write and how to help them improve their writing than is usually acknowledged in classroom practice or in school curricula. Research continues to add to this store of knowledge at an increasingly rapid rate. In this section we present a sampling of research on writing in the elementary grades.

Delving into the ever-growing storehouse of research about student writing may not at first appear to satisfy a classroom teacher's almost insatiable desire to know "how to do it" in his or her classroom tomorrow morning. Yet examination and study of this research are essential for determining not only what one can do productively in a classroom setting but also why certain things ought to be done at certain points by way of instruction. Whether one starts with this quick sampling of research or skips ahead to Parts II and III of this book, to return to this part later, is not important; however, it is essential to study the results of this research at some point prior to deciding what to do in a specific classroom situation.

The three articles included here are intended only to alert teachers to the kinds and amount of research that exists on children's writing. Follow-up examination of the studies or sources cited in each article will be useful to educators who wish to explore in greater depth what researchers are finding out about how youngsters learn to write and about what is involved in the writing process.

The articles that follow move from a survey of research in writing to a survey of classroom practice in the use of writing in elementary school social studies and finally to a specific classroom study that integrates the two areas and presents specific implications for the study and teaching of writing. Although the article written by Carol Vukelich and Joanne Golden was published earlier in Childhood Education, it is so relevant to the purpose of this volume we elected to republish it here. Vukelich and Golden examined what research in general reveals about beginning writers; their report suggests numerous important implications for teachers. Bob Gilstrap's chapter reports what some elementary school teachers around the country are currently doing with writing in the social studies. Finally, Susan Florio and Joyce Howard Frank describe in detail how one teacher's use of writing in elementary school social studies illustrates the findings of writing research. The implications of each report for teachers are significant.

Considerable other research on writing exists. References to some of this research can be found in the bibliography of ERIC resources which concludes this book.

1. THE DEVELOPMENT OF WRITING IN YOUNG CHILDREN: A REVIEW OF THE LITERATURE

By Carol Vukelich and Joanne Golden

Recent research in writing has shifted in emphasis from analysis of the written product to investigation of the writing process, in focus from the writing of older children to the writing of younger children, and from an emphasis on studying how children acquire the tool of writing (handwriting) to an effort to determine how young children acquire an understanding of writing as a means of communication. The findings of these investigations have direct implications for how the classroom teacher should approach the teaching of writing with young children. The following sections summarize these findings and identify implications for the classroom teacher.

The Writing Process

Research on the writing process reflects an important shift from a focus on the written product to a focus on the writing process. Many recent researchers have categorized the writing process according to three stages: prewriting, writing (or composing), and rewriting.[1]

--The prewriting stage involves preparation for writing and includes intention, planning, and organization. Essentially, the writer thinks through the writing task.

--The composing stage is characterized by the actual writing of the text, which involves a complex process of developing the topic and making a number of decisions about form and content. During this stage, the writer does not write continuously; he or she pauses, rereads what has been written, and rewrites. Research indicates that different patterns are evident in good and poor writers at this stage. Good writers have more pauses, which are used for the planning, reorienting, and revising

---

of the writing, while less-able writers have fewer pauses which are less purposeful; for example, glancing around.[2]

--In the rewriting stage the writer rewrites, alters, confirms, or develops his or her writing.

Development of Understanding of Written Language

In their efforts to discover when children develop an understanding of written language, researchers have sought to determine at what age children demonstrate understanding of the graphic form of written language and when they demonstrate understanding of writing as a means of communicating with an audience.

At least three recent studies found that young nonreading children had acquired some basic understanding about the graphic form of written language. While it appears that 3-year-olds can distinguish pictures from writing, they cannot discriminate between a word and single letters, consonant clusters, vowel clusters, words with disoriented letters, and abbreviations.[3] According to researchers, this skill of discriminating words from nonwords does not appear until sometime between the ages of 5 and 6.[4]

A component of the research by Graves, Sowers, and Calkins, as reported by Calkins, focused on when children demonstrate understanding of writing as a means of communication.[5] Their research suggests that children's early writing efforts resemble play in that there is no planning and no goal. Only later, with the onset of concern for conventions (for example, correct punctuation and spelling and proper letter formation), do children evidence development toward writing as a means of communicating with an eventual audience. Children at this stage show their understanding of writing as a means of communication through (1) wanting the paper to be legible, (2) choosing topics on the basis of audience, (3) being concerned with correctness and conventions, (4) anticipating audience response and needs, and (5) looking back on the writing.[6]

Acquisition of Writing Skills

Several researchers--Graves, Calkins, Wheeler, and Clay--have examined the behaviors children demonstrate as they acquire skill in writing.[7] Through videotapes, observation notes, and photocopies of children's writing, Graves and Calkins reported the following generalizations about young writers:

--The stages of writing (prewriting, writing, and rewriting) are evident in first-grade children, although there is considerably less rewriting at this age.

--As children try writing with more complexity, they give less attention to syntax, spelling, and punctuation.

--When choosing a topic to write about, first-graders typically choose to write a narrative.

--Children do not always begin with a clear idea of what they will write about.[8]

--Children progress from putting titles under drawings, to writing sentences that label their artwork, to writing more as printing becomes easier.

--By grade 2 most children have progressed from letters to words and from words to phrases and episodes, characteristically linked together by a string of ands.[9]

Calkins's work lends support to the earlier work by Wheeler, who reported that children's writing progresses from scribbles to designs to pictures, and then to letters, words in isolation, word phrases, and words in sentences.[10]

Clay developed one of the more detailed analyses of young children's writing.[11] In observing the writing of 5-year-olds in New Zealand, Clay noted 11 general principles and concepts in the writing of young children. At varying points, children demonstrated awareness that writing was a sign, that it carried a message, and that it had certain conventions such as spacing. Clay discovered that children experiment with writing, testing flexibility of symbols, making inventories of what they know, generating lines with a few symbols, and contrasting letters and words.

Beginning Spelling Strategies

Because strategies used by young children to spell are integral components of the beginning writing process, any summary of recent literature on acquisition of writing skills in young children would be incomplete without a section on early spelling strategies.

Since 1970 a number of researchers have indicated interest in children's beginning spelling strategies. Charles Read is known for significant contributions to this area.[12] By observing early writers, Read found that some children began writing as young as age 3½, usually before they could read but after they had learned conventional names for letters of the alphabet. Read found that young children spell according to their own perceptions of the phoneme/grapheme correspondences, which are different from adult perceptions. Children spell according to the point of articulation of the sound. This leads to patterns that include omitting medial nasals (boppie/bumpy), using ch and j in place of t and d before r (chray/tray; jragn/dragon), and switching lax vowels (fes/fish). Read identified at least six patterns in children's invented spellings which reflect their systematic and logical approach to spelling.

Subsequent investigations by Beers, Henderson et al., Sorenson and Kerstetter, Gentry, and Beers and Beers have extended the use of Read's strategies to children of various ages and from various environments.[13] Accumulating evidence strongly suggests that changes in spelling strategies used by children occur sequentially and systematically over an extended period of time. The pattern, according to Beers and Beers, appears to be affected by the child's level of cognitive development rather than by the reading or spelling instructional procedures employed in the classroom.[14]

Influence of the Environment

It could be hypothesized that children's understanding of the writing process may be influenced by their exposure to writing in their environment. A study by Lavine strongly suggests that the opportunity to observe print is important to children's understanding of the graphic form of written language.[15] Mexican children from a nonprint-oriented environment were less able to discriminate pictures from writing that Mexican children from print-oriented environments. To date, this is the only study to report on the effect of the cultural environment on the writing process.

Likewise, studies that explore the effect of writing in the home environment on understanding of the writing process and development of writing skills are few in number. Those which have considered the role of parents in early writing indicate that early writers observed family members engaged in writing activities and had books and materials available to them. In addition, many of the parents responded to questions about writing.[16] Few parents engaged in direct instruction, and most maintained that children picked up writing on their own.[17]

Graves examined writing role models in the school environment and discovered that children have few models in school.[18] He contended that teachers do not perceive themselves as writers and that they do not see the significance of role modeling in writing. It appears that educators not only do not perceive the importance of writing with children, they also do not recognize the importance of providing children with opportunities to write.[19] Indeed, Shanahan reported that the teachers in his survey indicated confusion about their role in writing and in instruction in writing.[20]

Implications for Teachers

The majority of research findings reported in this article date from 1970. Though research in the development of writing in young children is in the early stages, the accumulating data have these important implications for the classroom teacher:

--Focus on the writing process, rather than on the written product, and emphasis on the three stages of writing should affect the classroom teacher's work with children.

--Teachers will want to provide children with opportunities to engage in appropriate activities during all three stages of writing.

--Children must be provided with time and guidance to permit planning of the writing.

--Rethinking during the writing stage should be encouraged; time should be allowed for reflection and decision making.

--Because rewriting is an integral component of the writing process, evaluation of the product should be a joint teacher/child effort.

--Children should be provided with opportunities to rewrite or revise their products.

--An effective teacher will provide time for all three stages to occur naturally in the classroom and will guide children in development of all three kinds of writing skills.

If, as research indicates, very young children's awareness of the writing process is that writing is play without goal or planning, then teachers must provide young children with opportunities to engage in writing as play behavior. In essence, recent literature is suggesting that teachers whose current beginning writing activities emphasize the teacher in the role of scribe, with children merely copying the written message, need to expand the writing activities provided for children. Children need opportunities to think and write independently. For most early childhood teachers, this approach represents a significant deviation from their current practices. As children progress in the primary grades, emphasis on correctness and conformity to standard conventions (for example, letter formation, spelling, and form) should be delayed until the children develop an understanding of writing as a means of communicating with an audience. Even when it becomes appropriate to introduce writing with conventions, the teacher will want the children to do the revising, with some guidance and assistance.

In evaluating children's written products and interpreting early writing behaviors, it is important for teachers to know that young children progress from writing as play to writing as a means of communication; that they progress from scribbles to designs, then to pictures, letters, words, phrases, and finally sentences; and that in acquiring writing skills they demonstrate certain principles. Knowing what behaviors to expect of children will help the teacher support and foster children's natural development of writing skills.

Current findings on beginning spelling strategies challenge teachers to rethink their approach to the teaching of spelling. Data suggest that children test out their own system of matching letters and sounds when they attempt to spell and that they will learn adult spelling patterns if they are given many experiences with the written language. Hence, rather than direct instruction in spelling, young children should be given numerous opportunities to test out their sound/symbol generalizations, to revise their generalizations, and eventually to acquire adult spelling patterns through a natural process.

It appears that exposure to writing is a critical component in the development of writing abilities. In home, school, and cultural environments, young children need opportunities to observe print. The teacher will want to prepare a classroom for young children with signs, labels, messages, books, and other written materials--an environment rich in opportunities to observe print. Further, the teacher will want to alert parents to the importance of the role of written messages in acquiring an understanding of the written language.

In addition to viewing samples of print, young children need opportunities to observe family members and teachers who are engaged in writing activities. Teachers and parents must perceive themselves as writers and serve as writing models for children in classroom or home. This is one way that teachers and parents can demonstrate the purpose of writing as a communication tool.

When provided with written materials, parents who engaged in writing activities, and parents who answered their questions, some children learned to write without direct instruction. Perhaps teachers need to question the amount of time spent in direct instruction in writing in relation to the amount of time children are provided with instruction through observation of writing models.

In summary, recent research in the development of writing skills has many important implications for teachers. A knowledgeable teacher can do much to foster writing growth in young children and to plan a supportive writing environment for them.

Notes

1. See Janet Emig, "The Composing Processes of Twelfth-Graders," NCTE Research Report no. 13 (Urbana, Ill.: National Council of Teachers of English, 1971), ED 058 205; Charles Stallard, "Composing: A Cognitive Process Theory," College Composition and Communication 27 (1976), pp. 181-84, EJ 144 526; Donald Murray, "Internal Revision: A Process of Discovery," in Charles Cooper and Lee Odell, eds., Research on Composing: Points of Departure (Urbana, Ill.: National Council of Teachers of English, 1978); J.I. Britton et al., The Development of Writing Abilities (London: Macmillan, 1975); Donald Graves, "Children's Writing: Research Directions and Hypotheses Based Upon an Examination of the Writing Processes of Seven-Year-Old Children" (doctoral dissertation, 1973), ED 095 586.

2. Sharon Pianko, "Reflection: A Critical Component of the Composing Process," College Composition and Communication 30 (1978), pp. 275-78; also see Graves, "Children's Writing."

3. Linda Lavine, "Development of Differentiation of Letter-like Forms in Pre-reading Children," Child Development, 1972; Elfrieda H. Hiebert, "Preschool Children's Understanding of Written Language," Child Development 49 (December 1978), pp. 1231-34.

4. Celia A. Brownell et al., "Young Children's Knowledge of Word Structure," Child Development 49 (September 1978), pp. 669-680.

5. Lucy McCormick Calkins, "Children Learn the Writer's Craft," Language Arts 57 (February 1980), pp. 207-213.

6. Calkins, "Children Learn," pp. 211.

7. See Donald Graves, "Balance the Basics: Let Them Write," *Learning*, April 1978, pp. 30-33, EJ 186 141; M.E. Wheeler, "Untutored Acquisition of Writing Skill" (doctoral dissertation, Cornell University, 1971); Marie Clay, *What Did I Write?* (Auckland: Heinemann, 1975); Lucy McCormick Calkins, "Learning to Throw Away," *Language Arts* 56 (October 1979), pp. 747-752.

8. Graves, "Balance the Basics."

9. Calkins, "Learning to Throw Away."

10. Wheeler, "Untutored Acquisition."

11. Clay, *What Did I Write?*

12. Charles Read, "Preschool Children's Knowledge of English Phonology," *Harvard Educational Review* 41 (1971), pp. 1-34; Read, *Children's Categorization of Speech Sounds in English* (Urbana, Ill.: National Council of Teachers of English, 1975), ED 112 426.

13. James Wheelock Beers, "First- and Second-Grade Children's Developing Concepts of Tense and Lax Vowels" (doctoral dissertation, 1974); Edmund H. Henderson, Thomas H. Estes, and Susan Stonecash, "An Exploratory Study of Word Acquisition Among First-Graders at Midyear in a Language Experience Approach," *Journal of Reading Behavior* 4 (Summer 1972), pp. 21-31; Marilou R. Sorenson and Kristen Jeffers Kerstetter, "Phonetic Spelling: A Case Study," *Language Arts* 56 (October 1979), pp. 798-803; Richard J. Gentry, "Early Spelling Strategies," *Elementary School Journal* 79 (November 1978), pp. 88-92; James Wheelock Beers and Carol Strickland Beers, "Vowel Spelling Strategies Among First and Second-Graders: A Growing Awareness of Written Words," *Language Arts* 57 (February 1980), pp. 166-171.

14. Beers and Beers, "Vowel Spelling Strategies."

15. Cited in Eleanor G. Gibson and Harry Levin, *The Psychology of Reading* (Cambridge: Massachusetts Institute of Technology Press, 1975).

16. Mary Anne Hall, Sara A. Moretz, and Jodellano Statom, "Writing Before Grade One: A Study of Early Writers," *Language Arts* 53 (May 1976), pp. 582-85; Read, "Preschool Children's Knowledge."

17. C. Hildreth, "Developmental Sequences in Name Writing," *Child Development*, 1936, pp. 291-303.

18. Graves, "Balance the Basics."

19. Graves, "Balance the Basics"; Timothy Shanahan, "The Writing Crisis: A Survey and a Solution," *Phi Delta Kappan* 61, no. 3 (November 1979), pp. 216-17, EJ 210 997.

20. Shanahan, "The Writing Crisis."

2. WRITING IN ELEMENTARY SCHOOL SOCIAL STUDIES: REPORT OF A PERSONAL SEARCH

By Robert Gilstrap

During the summer of 1978 I began a personal search to learn more about how writing was being used in current elementary school social studies programs.[1] As a teacher educator whose primary interests are in elementary social studies and language arts, I was invited to serve on the staff of a summer institute sponsored by the Northern Virginia Writing Project, a spinoff of the Bay Area Writing Project. One of my summer responsibilities was to develop a workshop presentation introducing teachers to ways in which writing could be effectively used in elementary school social studies.

As an initial step in preparing the workshop, I developed a list of opportunities for writing in elementary school social studies. To do this, I first reviewed the course guides, lesson plans, and textbooks that I had recently used with my students and listed the types of writing I was encouraging them to include in their social studies units. I then reviewed other recent undergraduate social studies methods textbooks in my professional library to discover what additional writing activities could be added. Finally, I interviewed several elementary school teachers to get their reactions to the list of activities I was developing and their suggestions.

As I reviewed my list of writing activities, I discovered that all of them could be classified under one of the general phases of a unit of instruction, which are: (1) planning and initiating, (2) gathering information, (3) using and sharing information, and (4) culminating and evaluating. As a handout for my presentation, I developed a list of the most commonly recommended activities under each of these phases (see Figure 1). This list documents the many opportunities that exist to involve children in meaningful writing activities in elementary school social studies. Although writing was not viewed by many of the writers of texts for teachers or for children as of primary importance in a good social studies program, most authors did include some writing activities. As one might

Figure 1

RECOMMENDED SOCIAL STUDIES WRITING ACTIVITIES

1. Planning and Initiating

--completing preassessment exercise and tests

--preparing contracts

--developing questions to be answered during the unit

--doing initial data gathering for the purpose of determining what to study

--preparing questions for a resource person who will help initiate the unit

2. Gathering Information

--taking notes

--summarizing

--outlining

--observing and describing

--recording answers to interview questions

--keeping diaries and logs of reactions and insights

--writing letters for information

3. Using and Sharing

--writing reports

--writing plays and stories

--developing scripts for slide presentations

--developing learning centers

--preparing bulletin boards

--writing dialogue for cartoons

--making maps

--preparing time lines

--making charts

--writing book reviews

--developing historical newspapers, diaries, and letters

--writing lyrics to songs

--writing itineraries for imaginary trips

4. Culminating and Evaluating

--developing personal summaries of progress to accompany children's work (e.g., "Things I've Learned" booklets)

--drawing conclusions from the unit

--responding to problem situations related to the content of the unit

--selecting questions for future units on basis of knowledge gained from this one

--listing, defining, and responding to questions

--using checklists and rating scales for self-evaluation

expect, however, the emphasis on reading was much greater than the emphasis on writing.

During the last week of the summer institute, I finally had the opportunity to give my presentation. I shared my findings from the early part of my search with the teachers and gave them the opportunity to share with me some of the specific activities that they had found successful. I asked them to complete five-by-eight-inch cards on which they described their most effective writing activity in the area of social studies. We shared these during the workshop, and most of the activities mentioned fell under the third category on my chart. I asked them if I could have their cards so I could use them during future workshops. Most of the teachers were pleased to share their ideas with me.

Because of the interaction among teachers which I had planned as part of the workshop, the presentation was well received, and I was asked to conduct the workshop several times during the following year. Each time I asked the teachers to complete cards, and each time category three appeared to be the one most often mentioned as I read through the cards.

In the fall of 1979, I was asked to present my workshop on writing in the elementary school social studies at a state social studies weekend conference, and again the cards were distributed and effective uses of writing were recorded.

On Monday morning when I returned to my university office, I pulled out the stack of index cards that I had collected at the state meeting and placed it on my work table. As I read through the new set of cards, I sorted them into four stacks, one for each of the categories on my chart. Again one stack was noticeably thicker--the one for phase three, using and sharing information. My informal study of elementary teachers in Virginia was clearly revealing that, when asked to identify the most effective writing activity involving social studies, approximately 75 percent described an activity that took place near the end of a unit of instruction. On the basis of the research that I had done in preparing the list of writing opportunities for my workshop handout, this seemed to be a very narrow use of writing. I was curious to know whether this limited use of writing was typical of teachers in other parts of the nation, so I decided to expand my local search by doing a national survey of teachers. I selected as my sample for the survey those elementary teachers who had participated in summer institutes of the National Writing Project.

My first step was to write to the directors of all of the National Writing Project sites. At that time there more than 70. I gave each director a description of my study and asked for a list of all the elementary school teachers who had participated in summer institutes since the projects began. As a result of these requests, I received more than 300 names.

I then wrote to these teachers asking them to complete a questionnaire which included the following major requests:

1. In an average week, how much time is spent on writing activities in your social studies program?

2. In general, what kinds of writing activities do you use in or plan for your class in the area of social studies (research reports, book reports, interviews, etc.)?

3. Describe in detail the social studies writing activity that you have found to be most effective with your children. (This should be a description of one of the types of activities listed under question 2. If available, attach a sample assignment or work sheet.)

The enthusiasm for writing expressed by many who responded was amazing. Sixty-four teachers completed the questionnaire and enclosed notes related to their interest in the results of the study as well as samples of children's writings and artwork. By the spring of 1981, my office was filled with evidence that a great deal of writing was going on in elementary school social studies--at least in the classrooms of teachers who had been involved in the National Writing Project. During the summer, I completed my analysis of all the responses to the three major questions.

In reviewing the responses to question 1, which asked about the amount of time spent on social studies writing activities during an average week, I learned that the average among the 64 teachers who responded was 30 minutes per week. The responses ranged from "one-quarter hour" (two responses) to "five to seven hours a week in social studies as broadly defined" (one response). Quite a range! Although eight of the teachers were unable to determine how much time they actually spent on social studies writing activities because of the integrated nature of their curricula, the most-frequently mentioned response (10) was "one hour a week." The second-most-frequently mentioned response (6) was "one-half hour." Of the 64 teachers who responded to the survey, only 5 indicated that their students did either no writing or very little writing in the social studies.

The responses to question 2, which asked the teachers to identify the general kinds of social studies writing activities they used, revealed a varied set of writing opportunities that could be classified under all four categories. By the time that I had analyzed all of the survey forms, I had a list of 102 distinctive social studies activities that involved writing. The most frequently mentioned (33 responses) was some form of research paper or report. The next highest (14 responses) was book reports. Receiving five or more responses were letters, poems, paragraphs, short plays, stories, interviews, class notes, diaries, outlines, summaries of material read, essays, and essay questions.

I then classified each distinctive activity under the four categories mentioned earlier, using my original list as a guide for placement. My tally sheet looked like this:

1. Planning and initiating: 1 response
2. Gathering information: 19 responses
3. Using and sharing information: 70 responses
4. Culminating and evaluating: 12 responses

These results surprised me because I had carefully worded the second question so that those responding would have the opportunity to develop a list of activities that would reveal the range of writing in their classrooms. Again, the "using and sharing" category dominated the responses. These results supported the informal study that I had done during my workshops in Virginia, which had revealed that writing activities falling under this classification are the ones most often associated by elementary school teachers with social studies.

I should point out, however, that the list of 102 activities which emerged from the answers to this question included 54 activities that were not on the chart that I developed. I have listed some of these here:

--"We do a complete genealogy workup on each child. They conclude by writing a letter to their oldest known relative--bringing them up to date on the family." (fourth grade)

--"Writing questions and answers as a review of material studied. This is used in a game called 'Stump the Panel' in preparation for a test." (fifth grade)

--"News reports and commentaries that are aired on our school's closed-circuit TV station." (third/fourth grade)

--"I plant questions in bottles and jars all around the room before our day starts. The questions are about our current social studies unit. As children discover them, they open them, read the question, and write a response for me." (first grade)

--"Writing activities for a simulation are popular in my room. One example would be writing a script for a TV interview show with famous characters in U.S. history." (fifth grade)

--"Writing brief reviews of movies, books, speakers, field trips." (fourth grade)

--"Making and designing posters." (first grade)

--"Writing 'What Do You Think?' position papers." (fifth grade)

--"I assign some first-person reports, asking students to write from the viewpoint of a character from our social studies text." (fourth grade)

--"Recipe writing." (third grade)

--"Interviews of famous or not-so-famous people." (fourth grade)

--"We've done stories on how it feels to be handicapped based on a simulated experiment my students were involved in during which they were fixed up with a handicap for a day." (sixth grade)

--"We've written 'We're not so happy with you' letters to the secretary of the interior, who wants to lift the ban on importing whale products as well as other local, state, and national leaders." (kindergarten)

--"Writing advertisements for inventions (cotton gin, telephone, radio)." (fifth grade)

--"Writing jokes, riddles, and puns about social studies content." (fifth grade)

I next turned to the section of the survey which asked the teachers to describe in detail the social studies writing activity that they believed to be most effective and to include sample assignments or work sheets. I first tried to list each activity as a separate item, but I soon realized that many of the teachers had described their most effective writing activities in such detail that their descriptions often included experiences with writing which could fall under more than one of the four major categories that I had identified. I then decided to analyze each description carefully and to categorize each of the activities under one of the four headings. I soon realized that I needed to add a fifth category for non-unit-related activities. For example, one third-grade teacher wrote: "In third grade, the students do a very good job of writing about their feelings. They are not as inhibited as older children. I ask them to write how they feel when they are happy or surprised."

Reading through the descriptions of social studies writing activities, with the accompanying materials and pictures, was a real pleasure. It was obvious that some very exciting and effective learning experiences involving writing were being provided for children in these classes. Several people commented that it was impossible to describe the "most" effective activity, but that they could describe "an activity that worked"--and they did that very well. In the responses to this question, I was able to see the value given to writing activities that went beyond the using and sharing category.

After I finished reading all the descriptions, my tally sheet looked like this:

1. Planning and initiating: 8 activities
2. Gathering information: 39 activities
3. Using and sharing information: 43 activities
4. Culminating and evaluating: 9 activities
5. Non-unit-related: 4 activities

Although the number of activities that fall under "using and sharing information" again dominated the results, the responses for "gathering information" were very close behind with 39. "Initiating and planning" activities and "culminating and evaluating" activities almost balance out: eight for the first and nine for the second. Four people mentioned activities that from their descriptions could only be classified as non-unit-related.

By the fall of 1981, I had analyzed all my questionnaires. As I looked over my summary sheets, I asked myself: "What have I really learned from my study, and how can I use what I've learned to help other teachers, especially my undergraduate teachers-in-training?"

First, writing is used by a significant number of the elementary school social studies teachers who were surveyed. Of the 64 teachers who responded to my questionnaire, only 5 indicated that they did no or little writing as part of their social studies program.

Second, the survey reveals the variety of social studies writing activities that the teachers use in their social studies programs: 102 distinctive activities were tallied. Although I was disturbed to see that so many of these activities were limited to "using and sharing" information, when the teachers were asked to describe their most effective activities, writing activities that were used during earlier stages of a social studies unit were often identified.

Finally, even teachers who are interested in writing and who are knowledgeable about current information related to that process do not use writing to its fullest potential as a tool for communicating and thinking in elementary school social studies.

I believe that the results of this study have important implications. Future teachers need to better understand the significant role that writing can play as a tool for communicating and thinking as part of an effective social studies program. They need to be acquainted with current knowledge about how writing contributes to personal learning, a concept that is summarized as follows in a recent publication from the National Council of Teachers of English entitled Perspectives on Writing in Grades 1-8:[2]

> Personal learning values of writing stem from discovery. Through seeing personal ideas and experiences appear on paper, redrafting what is written to make it more accurate or complete, and receiving reader feedback on what has been written, a writer expands what is learned from the original experience. Being involved in, and yet in a sense detached from, experiences that have been recorded on paper encourages insight and discovery.

Teachers-in-training also need to better understand the many opportunities to use writing within a classroom, both unit-related and non-unit-related. Susan Florio, codirector of the Written Literacy Project at Michigan State University and coauthor of the third chapter in this book, with her colleague, Christopher M. Clark, recently studied the writing that is undertaken in a second/third-grade combination classroom and a sixth-grade classroom. As a result of their study, Florio and Clark identified the following general functions of writing in the classroom: (1) writing to know oneself and others, (2) writing to occupy free time, (3) writing to participate in the community, and (4) writing to demonstrate academic competence. Figure 2 gives a clearer picture of these functions.

Susan Florio and her colleagues have learned through their research that a great deal of writing does occur in the classroom and that much of it is enabled by teacher thought and action. They point out in their preliminary report that "lacking the props and constraints of other of the 'basic skill' areas, writing is often 'invisible' as teachers report their instructional lives or as researchers seek evidence of 'writing instruction'--or even as children or parents talk about the writing done in school. Writing in everyday school life may be 'invisible' in the sense that talk is invisible in everyday life--it is such a part of day-to-day transaction (tests, worksheets, essays, notes, letters, etc.) that it is taken for granted."[3] Their findings appear to support what I have learned through my study of the use of writing in the elementary school social studies curriculum.

Teachers-in-training also need more opportunities to write in ways that they will be asking their pupils to write in their social studies classes. Some authorities believe that the most effective teachers of writing are those who are writers themselves and who continually use writing in ways that their students are expected to do. Teachers-in-training need to develop confidence in using writing for many purposes.

Finally, future teachers need to become familiar with creative methods such as those described in this book. Many of the articles in this volume were written by elementary school teachers who were identified through my questionnaire. Knowing that inservice teachers are including effective writing activities in their social studies programs should give future teachers the support they need to give a higher priority to writing in the social studies.

Figure 2

THE FUNCTIONS OF WRITING AND THEIR DISTINCTIVE FEATURES

FUNCTION TYPE	SAMPLE ACTIVITY	DISTINCTIVE FEATURES						
		INITIATOR	COMPOSER	WRITER/ SPEAKER	AUDIENCE	FORMAT	FATE	EVALU-ATION
TYPE I: WRITING TO PARTICIPATE IN COMMUNITY	2/3 classroom rules	teacher	teacher & students	teacher	class-mates	by teacher and students: jointly rendered rules are drafted on chalkboard; printed in colored marker on large white paper by teacher	posted; referred to when broken	no
	6 magazines	teacher	teacher & students	student	magazine subscribers	by teacher; she provides magazines of former students as models	read by teacher; may be displayed for reading by classmates; taken home	yes
TYPE II: WRITING TO KNOW ONESELF AND OTHERS	2/3 diaries	teacher	student	student	self	by teacher; she models from literature and oversees making of the diaries. Students write or print on lined paper in booklets they have made	kept in teacher's file cabinet or in student desks; occasionally shared with teacher, other students, or family	no
	6 life books	teacher	teacher & students	student	class-mates	by teacher; her own work is used as a model	read by teacher, classmates, parents, other students	yes
TYPE III: WRITING TO OCCUPY FREE TIME	2/3 stories, letters, and cards	student	student	student	other (parents, friends, family)	by student; printed or drawn on lined or construction paper	kept; may be given as gift to parent or friend	no
	6 cartoons & stories	student	student	student	self or others (parents, friends, family)	by student: written or drawn on notebook paper, may be recopied	kept; may be shared or not be shared; when shared, it is usually with a friend.	no
TYPE IV: WRITING TO DEMONSTRATE ACADEMIC COMPETENCE	2/3 science lab booklets	teacher	publisher	publisher and student	teacher	by publisher: printed in commercial booklet in which students also write	checked by teacher; filed for later use; pages sent home to parents by teacher	yes
	6 research project	teacher	teacher & students	teacher & students	teacher & class-mates	by teacher: students draft their research project on dittoed outline & note sheets	read by teacher: presented orally to classmates; displayed at teacher conference	yes

Notes

1. In developing this article, I have attempted to use the process and format of an "I-Search Paper" as described by Ken Macrorie in his book Searching Writing (Rochelle Park, N.J.: Hayden Book Co., 1980). In an I-Search paper, the writer tells the story of what he or she did in the search and includes the following information: (1) what the writer knew or didn't know about the topic when starting out, (2) why the paper is being written, (3) the story of the search, and (4) what was or was not learned from the search.

2. Shirley Haley-James, Perspectives on Writing in Grades 1-8 (Urbana, Ill.: National Council of Teachers of English, 1981), p. 5.

3. Christopher M. Clark and Susan Florio, Understanding Writing in School: A Descriptive Study of Writing and Its Instruction in Two Classrooms, final report of the Written Literacy Study (East Lansing, Mich.: Institute for Research on Teaching, Michigan State University, 1981).

3. LITERACY AND COMMUNITY IN THE CLASSROOM: A CASE STUDY OF BETTERBURG

By Susan Florio and Joyce Howard Frank

In 1977-1978, two researchers from the Institute for Research on Teaching conducted a study of the teaching and learning of writing in Joyce Frank's second-grade classroom in the small Michigan town of Haslett.[1] These researchers observed Mrs. Frank and her students as they engaged in a variety of activities, many of which involved writing.[2] They got to know the members of the class, provided help when asked, joined in class activities, made videotapes of some lessons, and asked many questions of both Mrs. Frank and her students during formal interviews and informal conversations. This article shares some of what was learned about the acquisition of written literacy as it takes place in Mrs. Frank's classroom community. What happens here may well be typical of the development of writing as it occurs in second-grade classrooms. Knowing this information can be most useful to teachers who are planning to use writing in elementary school social studies.

Setting the Scene

To get to Mrs. Frank's second-grade classroom, you must travel to the small community of Haslett, Michigan. This town of nearly 7,000 people is located in the shadow of the state capital and Michigan State University. Although some of the residents are farmers, most of the children in Mrs. Frank's room have parents employed in one of the area's major activities--state government, education, or manufacturing.

Mrs. Frank's students attend the Ralya School, one of the three elementary schools in Haslett. The one-story contemporary school building houses about 170 students and contains one room for each grade from kindergarten through fifth. Upon entering Mrs. Frank's classroom, one encounters yet another small community--one which the children have dubbed "Betterburg."

The members of Mrs. Frank's class populate Betterburg. They fill its civic offices and devise its laws. Betterburg contains all the components that one would expect in a small community--law enforcement, cultural activities, commerce, a bank, social welfare, a library, and a postal system. Of course, Betterburg is also a schoolroom, and as such it contains other such standard features as blackboards, desks, and bookshelves. But the dominance of the town is evidenced by the fact that the children, when asked upon leaving the room one day to draw maps of the important things and places in the room, overwhelmingly included each aspect of Betterburg. Often the buildings were drawn in considerable detail.

Literacy and Community: A Brief Review

Vygotsky has talked about learning to write as the acquisition of a "particular system of symbols and signs whose mastery heralds a critical turning point in the entire cultural development of the child."[3] Thus, when we ask questions about the acquisition of written literacy by children, it can be said that we are asking fundamental questions about both the individual psychological development of those children and their membership in a community. The acquisition of systems of signs and symbols in speaking, reading, and writing provides stunning examples of the interconnections between the growth of the individual and that of society. Schwab,[4] for example, in the essay "Learning Community," asserts that

> our beginning personness, as children, consists first of a world of perceived and felt significances that we have made from things seen. It is when another--adult or child--signals recognition that we have such a world, seeks to know it, and tries to give us a glimpse of his private world, that one-to-one community begins. This is done in one and only one way--through speech, by talk.

Speech and writing are both instances of the use of cultural tools--they are systems created and passed on in societies in order for the members of those societies to live and work meaningfully together.[5]

Thinking about writing in this way has implications for its instruction in school. Perhaps teachers can best serve the acquisition of writing by structuring both for and with students social occasions in which writing functions meaningfully as communication. This possibility parallels what we know about the acquisition of speaking, another complex communicative skill. Both research and experience tell us that spoken language is acquired literally "in the doing." Children are welcomed as communicators even before their first words are uttered. Early in life, children find that their moves and sounds elicit action from other people. Children, in effect, practice the use of language not as preparation or training for social life but as social life itself.

Research on language acquisition has shown us that requisite grammatical skills are seldom taught directly to children by the adults with whom they communicate. For teachers of writing, an essential lesson from research on language acquisition is that even the most flawed and rudimentary communicative attempts of novices are functional in that they have social meaning. Critical to acquiring language is the social fact that a child's emergent and stumbling efforts are heeded by others. Early talk is meaningful by virtue of the child's membership in the family, the first community.

Research in one traditional society where it is possible to separate the acquisition of written literacy from the formal school setting is also suggestive about the relation between the process of becoming a speaker and that of becoming a writer. Among the Vai in Liberia, where literacy in the native language is acquired informally, Goody and other researchers have described the process of becoming literate as one directly related to the conduct of everyday life.[6] The occasion for mastery of written symbols, much like the occasion for mastery of speech, arises in the course of social life and is supported by the community in which it occurs. People come to write because, within their community, they need to be able to perform the operations--both public and private--that written literacy makes possible. They need to engage in commerce or to keep records; they need to extend their social relations over time and distance; they need to mark formally important social occasions; they need to remind themselves of the thoughts they have had.

Viewed in this light, conventional expectations about the role of formal schooling in the acquisition of writing seems hopelessly out of joint with what transpires in traditional society or with the powerful language learning that takes place as speech is acquired in our own families. One of the distinctive features of a school is that it is intentionally special. It is a place set apart by the society precisely for the transmission of cultural norms thought to enable adult membership in that society. Ironically, however, the special nature of the school virtually ensures its isolation from the mainstream of everyday community life in which adults function. Thus it is not surprising that a defining feature of school learning is its abstractness. Principles to be learned are isolated from the life situations in which they might be applied. Componential skills are isolated for practice and mastery, removed from both the complex processes of which they are a part and the purposes for which they might be undertaken. Yet the powerful assumption is made that mastery of such isolated principles and skills will enhance mature functioning in adult society--that skills will somehow "transfer" from school to everyday life situations.[7]

But classrooms contain the stuff of community, too, and therein lies the potential that writing done in them will be meaningful. Classrooms are located in organized social worlds where meanings are shared and values held, and at the same time classrooms individually constitute small communities with cumulative histories, shared beliefs, and rights and responsibilities of membership. The learning environment that Mrs. Frank and her students created in the form of Betterburg provides an opportunity to examine the relationship between literacy and community in the social context of the classroom.

A Closer Look at Betterburg

In the early days of the school year, all of the second-graders in Haslett study communities as part of their social studies curriculum. It is a natural followup to ask the students if the elements of community are available in their classroom. If so, would they like to see their classroom become a town, city, or suburb? Once the to-be-expected chorus of approval is voiced, again the natural followup is to explain that towns (cities) arise as the need for them arises. What will be the goal for their town? Together the students must plan and write this goal. They must work as city planners to plan their community. What public buildings are needed, and where should they be located? Students justify their plans by writing statements such as the following: "On my plan the bank is at the front [of the town] so everyone can see the robbers come" or "The police station is in the back corner so the kids in jail can't see what's going on" or "The library is next to the welfare office because if you've got to go to the welfare, you're feeling bad and a book will cheer you up."

Now that the planning is done, the city founders need to construct their town. Again they need to write--this time letters to carpenters, parents, or second-grade alumni asking them for help in the physical building of the community. Many of the written requests meet with success as parents, friends, and particularly former second-graders lend a hand in the construction of buildings of wood, cardboard, and paper.

When the buildings are constructed, the students need to learn how to use them. Again they write. This time letters are sent to civic officials--postmasters of Haslett and the United States, sheriffs, and the like. The letters inquire about the special buildings in which important civic functions are performed. Responses are often accompanied by invitations to visit and tour the local post office, police station, or bank. In addition, the replies students receive are typewritten on official embossed stationery. Each reply functions as the child's own private, individual "textbook," teaching the recipient what he or she needs to know in order to manage a particular building in the town.

As these activities are occurring early in the year, other parallel activities are going on. The students had learned earlier in social studies that communities have rules and government. Their town (city) needs rules as well, so the students elect three branches of government--federal, state, and local. Again, written literacy plays an important part in the establishment of community. Campaign speeches are written and elections are held. Each child is elected to an office and will receive leadership training, again by means of writing. The newly elected officials take pencils in hand and write for job training to their elected counterparts in the governments of the United States, Michigan, and Haslett. Again, each child receives an impressive letter in reply--but this time the people writing to them are people whom they have read and heard about! Governors, mayors, senators, and secretaries of state write informative letters that typically also include booklets, pictures, autographs, and materials that the students can use in their own official capacities; for example, badges, firefighter or postal worker hats, sheriffs' patches, and decals. Some requests for information motivate telephone calls from such Washington dignitaries as the United States treasurer and cabinet secretaries. Other requests find their way into the local newspaper as a result of contacts to the paper from the judges, legislators, or other officials to whom the children have written. Still others result in personal visits to the classroom from members of government.

By this time the town has come to life, but the students still need rules or laws. Each student writes a bill for a proposed rule that may be necessary for life in the classroom town. Legislative sessions are held by the newly elected officials, and the bills are amended and become laws. This activity provides students the opportunity to deliberate about community norms and reach consensus on the ways to express them. It culminates in the rendering of the rules "official," by their codification in public, written form.

Betterburg needs employees for its various civic and commercial activities, so the students write advertisements for the town's jobs and fill out applications to be hired for them. Once hired and gainfully "employed" as florists, clerks, store manager, janitor, pollution inspector, paint foreman, banker, and the like, the students are paid with the town currency. The town is functioning now, and still the writing continues. Each citizen's "job" includes record-keeping. The sheriff and police chief need to fill out the police blotter as they enforce the community's laws. The social welfare director needs to keep a record of the money given out. The postmaster needs to schedule her workers to sort and deliver the large amount of mail sent and received through the Betterburg post office. Bankers keep advanced records of financial transactions. The township clerk registers voters, oversees town voting, and records election results.

With the Betterburg post office now in working order, students correspond with each other, with other students in the school, and with family members. Letters are written during free-time periods, when work is completed, on rainy recesses, or at home in the evenings. Despite the fact that this is an unsupervised, unrequired writing activity, the output is large. Children write anywhere from two to ten letters per night to place in the post office for delivery the next morning. They are rewarded for their efforts when they receive a local reply from a classmate, "outstate" mail from another student in the school, or even a letter through the U.S. mail from a parent, relative, or neighbor.

Letter writing of all sorts can be observed almost daily over the months of Betterburg's existence, and when the children were interviewed at the end of the year about their activities by researchers, the only writing activity on which they commented in detail was that of writing letters. The following excerpts from the interviews are illustrative:

Interviewer:	I want to know about all the things you wrote this year.
Student 1:	Yeah, we wrote people to come to our store.
Student 2:	Letters.
Student 3:	Oh, yeah. We wrote to our moms and dads and wrote to kids in our class.
Student 4:	Our post office would get mail.

Additional evidence of the importance of letter writing in this classroom community can be found in the facts that the post office was among the places most frequently shown on students' classroom maps and that the mailboxes--both the one outside the post office and those fastened to the children's desks--were included in maps made by well over half the students. Finally, when Mrs. Frank and the students recorded the history of Betterburg in their yearbook, the text consisted almost entirely of the letters which had been written during the town's existence.

Eventually Betterburg develops commerce. When the students decide to have factories and a store, they write to companies asking to buy materials wholesale. One persuasive letter written to a games manufacturer requested that games be purchased at wholesale prices for sale in the Betterburg store. In addition, the commerce of Betterburg requires a bank loan to raise money for the initial purchase of wholesale goods. Once again the students find themselves in transaction with the adult world by means of the written word.

Many other types of writing accompany and enable commerce in Betterburg. To advertise the Betterburg store, students write jingles for posters, handbills, and a variety of different types of ads, including radio ads that rely solely on "word pictures" to convey their messages, television ads in which the students must decide what to show and describe, and newspaper ads where illustration is an important part of the message. They also prepare speeches for presentations to groups or to individuals in the community, along with letters of invitation and thanks. At a local department store, they are trained in sales by a store executive as an employee would be. They then write sample sales talks describing the value of their products following the outline he has given them.

The citizens of Betterburg are civic minded. Their efforts in Haslett have resulted in traffic lights, planter boxes, sidewalks, even the beginning of a cleanup of a nearby lake and recreation area. A proclamation written by the students to a local drain commissioner, honoring his efforts in the lake cleanup, was read and presented to the official by the citizens of Betterburg at the ceremonies marking the start of the dredging of the lake.

When students can write letters and, as a result, see a sidewalk where there was not one before or instigate the placement of a planter on a bare and ugly street corner, they may have learned a lesson about the power of written expression and about their own power and social responsibility.

Lessons from Betterburg

The celebration of community in Mrs. Frank's classroom in the form of Betterburg appears to be related powerfully to the practice of writing as an expressive activity in several ways. Betterburg affords immediate and explicit sharing of class membership to the students. As such, the town requires written records of that experience. The classroom town also provides, as we have seen in the example of the letters to manufacturers and civic officials, the occasion for students to venture outside the classroom walls into the wider adult community. This movement is a challenging one for the novice writer--one that requires diligence and a purpose. It constitutes, in the words of Elsasser and John-Steiner, a "critical shift in the consciousness of the learner, a shift of attention from an immediate audience that shares the learner's experience and frame of reference to a larger, abstract, and unfamiliar audience."[8]

The essential lesson for writing instruction that can be drawn from Betterburg is virtually the same lesson that can be drawn from the observation of first language acquisition or from the recent studies of the acquisition of cognitive skills in traditional societies. The lesson is not simply that skills are seldom taught directly in such contexts by those already expert in their use, but, more important, that even the most rudimentary attempts of novices are taken to have social functions. Critical to acquiring communicative skills is the condition that a child's emergent and stumbling efforts are heeded by others, and that early attempts at expression are meaningful by virtue of the child's membership in a community. In Betterburg, the most complex of writing activities--and the ones in which the most time is spent--transpire outside of the direct teaching of skills. We observe instead considerable practice of writing as it is done for community purposes. Gradually, by means of such practice, the children approximate the fully matured forms, with remediation being applied rarely and only as it serves to enhance each child's expressive intentions.

Betterburg is not an extracurricular activity, nor is it a "frill" in the school's busy day. It is the social context within which academic learning happens meaningfully. To be sure, a part of each day in Mrs. Frank's room is spent in the direct instruction of various skills involved in writing. But it is writing in use that occupies the foreground of student attention and action. If it is likely, in Scribner and Cole's words, "that there are some informal, everyday situations showing one or another feature of school learning,"[9] it can perhaps be hypothesized as well that, to the extent that any classroom constitutes a small community or transacts with the wider adult world, there will be features of informal learning within it. Betterburg presents such a situation in rather bold strokes, illustrating the enormous power of community in the acquisition of functional written literacy.

As children learn to read, write, and compute in the context of Betterburg, they are reinforced in a variety of ways. As we have seen, writing in Betterburg is reinforced in the following ways:

--Letters are written for a purpose, and there is the expectation and generally the receipt of a reply.

--Many written works are published, either within Betterburg itself or in the wider community.

--All writing is undertaken in the accomplishment of a task, and the tasks may vary in complexity from record-keeping to persuasion.

Betterburg offers evidence that there are many ways to reinforce student effort and that some of those ways reward students more richly because they engender values and enjoyment of writing as well as skill mastery. In Betterburg at the start of the year, very few children volunteer to undertake the writing tasks needed to get the town started. But within weeks, after the replies start rolling in, most children are eager to write because they know that something enjoyable and interesting will result.

Betterburg could not exist without literacy. Every job and civic office requires both bookkeeping of some sort and an opportunity to lead. At some point in the course of life in Betterburg, every student experiences having responsibility for his or her peers. As children "put on" the social roles of Betterburg, they have the opportunity both to shape and to be shaped by a social identity. No two Betterburg police officers are alike, for example, yet each child who is a police officer assumes some aspect of the putative role. For many children, this is a novel opportunity to experience personal growth and social responsibility in school. Such an opportunity to feel personally responsible and powerful, it has been argued, is integrally related to the acquisition of literacy.[10]

Despite the many benefits to be derived from such a classroom community, the already busy teacher may wonder about its feasibility. How much time does it take? Can it be done in other types of schools and communities? Is there an essence of Betterburg that can be applied elsewhere without the cardboard buildings? For those who wish to try to develop a classroom community, the answer is simple. Betterburg is infused into the fabric of the day and year. Although great effort is required to initiate the town, once it begins, its laws and institutions give it a life of its own. Students share in the record-keeping for their own learning; their written work and the many letters they receive enrich the curriculum--in effect, they take on much of the responsibility of the creation of their educational materials and documentation of their progress which has heretofore been exclusively the function of teachers and publishers.

The opportunities for curricular integration that Betterburg provides are appealing as well in a school day increasingly taxed to include both the basic skills and many other subjects. When it is possible to teach social studies, language arts, and mathematics in the same activity, efficiency is achieved. And to the extent that we have evidence that language is learned most effectively in the service of other enterprises rather than in isolation, enrichment is possible as well.

There are many aspects of life in Betterburg which can be adapted to life in other classrooms without the literal creation of a classroom town. It is possible, for example, for students to draft, deliberate, and codify their own laws. They may also have classroom or schoolwide postal systems.[11] It is possible for students to publish their written work--in class books read by peers and schoolmates, or more widely in newspapers, magazines, and books. Finally, any class can become involved in the life of its community--whether that community is a small town like Haslett, a suburb, or an urban neighborhood. Such involvement not only provides experiences in social action, it forces children to transact in the adult world--the world that requires and will require of them the basic skills of literacy.

Notes

1. Some of the work reported in this paper was presented at the annual meeting of the American Educational Research Association, San Francisco, April 11, 1979, and was published in Florio, "Learning to Write in the Classroom Community." The project described in this chapter was honored by the Joint Council on Economic Education as the best primary-grade economics program in 1980. The authors acknowledge the support of the Institute for Research on Teaching at Michigan State University, which sponsored the research on which this report is partially based under a contract from the Teaching Division, National Institute of Education. The authors would also like to acknowledge the cooperation of the Haslett (Michigan) Public Schools.

2. Susan Wildfong assisted Susan Florio in the observational study of Mrs. Frank's classroom. Her contributions to the study are acknowledged here.

3. L.S. Vygotsky, Mind in Society: The Development of Higher Psychological Processes (Cambridge, Mass.: Harvard University Press, 1978), p. 106.

4. J.J. Schwab, "Learning Community," Center Magazine 8, no. 3 (1975), pp. 31-32.

5. M. Cole and S. Scribner, "Introduction," in Vygotsky, Mind in Society, p. 3.

6. J. Goody, M. Cole, and S. Scribner, "Writing and Formal Operations: A Case Among the Vai," Africa 47, (1977), pp. 289-304.

7. S. Scribner and M. Cole, "Cognitive Consequences of Formal and Informal Education," Science 182 (1973), EJ 088 326, pp. 553-59.

8. N. Elsasser and V.P. John-Steiner, "An Interactionist Approach to Advancing Literacy," Harvard Educational Review 47 (August 1977), EJ 167 145, p. 358.

9. Scribner and Cole, "Cognitive Consequences," p. 556.

10. P. Friere, Cultural Action for Freedom, Monograph Series no. 1 (Cambridge, Mass.: Harvard Educational Review and Center for the Study of Development and Social Change, 1970).

11. J. Greene, "The Purposes and Strategies of Interactive Letter Writing in the Classroom" (paper presented at the annual meeting of the American Educational Research Association, Los Angeles, April 15, 1981).

II. DEVELOPING READINESS FOR WRITING

It is almost axiomatic now to assert that if we are to help students learn how to write well we must focus as much on the process of writing as on the products of that writing. Writing specialists divide this process into three major stages--prewriting, composing, and revising. Teachers can provide instruction during each of these stages which will improve the way students write as well as the quality of what they write. When such instruction is conducted in a subject area such as social studies, instead of in a "content-free" area, students can improve their learning of subject matter at the same time.

The prewriting stage of writing is probably the most important stage of writing for elementary school children, as it is for all beginning writers at any grade level or age. For it is at this stage that writers focus on something to write about and invent an idea worth communicating to others. Without attending to these two crucial tasks, student writing frequently becomes an aimless and frustrating search for something to say--and the products of that writing turn out to be confusing at best or meaningless at worst.

For elementary school teachers, attention to prewriting involves essentially two challenges: (1) creating a classroom climate supportive of student writing and (2) helping students discover something worthwhile to write about. In the articles presented here, experienced elementary school teachers describe practical classroom techniques for accomplishing both of these goals.

The first two articles here stress two important aspects of a classroom environment that nurtures and supports student writing. Wendy Giordano describes one way to create a classroom atmosphere that encourages primary-grade students to write and to share their writing with others. Barbara Meyer suggests some ways to use student writing to help students develop positive self-images, without which they are often reluctant to engage in or profit from instruction and practice in classroom writing. Judicious use of techniques such as these can go far toward developing the open, positive atmosphere in which student writing can grow and develop at any level.

Providing repeated opportunities for students to write and to see others write also constitutes part of a writing readiness program. Ada Marie Hooper explains how senior citizens can help assure that these goals can be achieved with primary- or intermediate-grade youngsters, while Mary McFarland describes the use of pictures to achieve these goals.

Deciding on something worth writing about is one of the initial and most difficult challenges facing any writer. Many techniques exist for helping youngsters meet this challenge. The remaining articles explain how some of these techniques can work with primary-grade children; with slight adaptation, they can also work with beginning writers of any age. Kristin Smyka explains how objects from the past may be used to stimulate students to write. Virginia Pfotenhauer illustrates classroom use of student brainstorming, and Beverly Chadburn explains a technique for generating vocabulary and ideas in writing.

Obviously, many other techniques can also be used to help students start writing. But familiarity with and use of the techniques described here can provide a core of classroom-tested techniques which teachers can use to prepare children to write in elementary school social studies.

4. CREATING A CLASSROOM CLIMATE FOR WRITING

By Wendy Giordano

Mike rushed into the room, his blond hair flying.

"Come on, you guys! We gotta write to the president. Somebody shot him!"

Within munutes Mike had transformed our typical morning free play into a writing group. As others came, they automatically joined in the writing. Some wrote, while others worked on the pictures that would accompany the writing they would do later.

> Dear Mr. President.
> Im sorry for you. my dad knows you do you know my dad. he road in a golf cart with you. im started soccer. the Pope gave my dad rosary beads my dad gave them to me. I hope you feel better.
> Love Tanya

> Dear Mr. President Reagan.
> I hope you feel good. my family is sad you got shot. a truck ranup my leg but my bone was not broken thet was a miracle the class is very very sad you got shot. God Loves me and you every day so he will hill you some day. You forgot to duck.
> From Samantha Grade One

I had been working with these 21 first-graders since September, and I had watched their enthusiasm for writing grow with secret pleasure. They obviously enjoyed writing. Teachers at some of my inservice presentations often asked how I was able to get children to love writing. They asked if this class was exceptional.

This class was more unusual than exceptional. The dozen children who presented discipline problems had sent me home after school in September feeling completely frustrated. Two students were from Vietnam and were learning English. Another child had qualified for the Learning Disabilities Resource Program, while one was physically handicapped. Nine of the students were repeating first grade. Their academic range was vast, from kindergarten reading readiness (one little girl spent the morning in kindergarten and the afternoon in first grade) to a test grade in the superior range for abstract reasoning. Yet perhaps it was this very mixture of ability and personality that resulted in rich and prolific writing!

For the last 12 years I had initiated the writing program sometime in the fall after my first-graders had mastered some basic routines. However, this year, Ngoc, my tiny, beautiful Vietnamese girl, had started in late September, before I thought we were really ready to begin.

"Do not cry, Steve!" she begged one day.

Steve was moving away so that he and his grandmother could have "a house with a yard with roses and a white fence." The class did not want Steve to move. His daily antics had endeared him to the others.

"We write to you," Ngoc exclaimed as she hugged him, shoving tissues into his hand.

After he moved, the children faithfully wrote to Steve. When after two months they had received no reply, they had a meeting.

"When you write you gotta get an answer or you quit writing," declared Eric. The decision was unanimous. Eric would write to Steve and explain why the class would not be writing anymore.

By writing letters, the children developed a sense of audience and peer-editing. The most important lesson they learned was that a response is necessary in order to have two-way communication. And so began the development of writing in my class of enthusiastic first-graders this past fall.

Meaningful student writing doesn't usually spring up unaided. It requires not only preparation on my part but readiness on the part of the children. However, what I do to help them get ready to write and then to support their writing plays a major role in making writing a natural part of our classroom.

Student writing requires a classroom climate of trust, openness, and support. Creating such a climate requires time and the cooperation of students and teacher alike. Over the years, I have used numerous techniques to build and maintain a climate supportive of writing.

For example, one early November morning we teachers were instructed to have our classes write about the return of the former hostages. Upon hearing this request I felt anxious, believing that the topic of the hostages in Iran was too advanced for first-graders. How wrong I was! As soon as I told them about the request, they became restless to talk as they sat crosslegged on the floor in front of me. The hum of their conversations grew louder and louder as they discussed what they knew about the topic. As always, some wrote while others worked on illustrations first. Many students vocalized as they worked. Terry would print a sentence and then put his pencil down, pick up his paper, and quietly read his entire work from the beginning.

"I go fast in my head and I don't want to leave stuff out," he explained to me.

Later that month I held a writing inservice meeting for other teachers. My pupils attended and participated by reading their hostage stories. I wanted to involve my class in a session where adults felt that writing, especially children's writing, was important. It was an emotion-packed session.

> Jessica. i am happy be Cause the hostages Are released and i am Happy be Cause the hostages Are going home Sweet home
>
> There was hostages in Iran. They aren't in Iran anymore. They are in Germany. The 52 Americans are in good condition. I am very very happy. The end. Dave
>
> Jeff. The hostages were Prisoners in Iran For a year 52 Then They Went to the airPort Then Up They Go In The Jat Zoom Zoom Zoom.

Children enjoy--and need--opportunities to share their writing with others in an atmosphere of support and appreciation. Parents can help provide such support, too. During the past year, social studies home-study units provided opportunities for students to complete various writing assignments with parent help. I gave my students dozens of suggestions for art projects, reading, and writing, and I requested them to complete one assignment a week. "Gee that was fun--we did something together and didn't end up fighting," commented one parent after he had spent time working on a project with his child. Parent involvement was one goal of my writing projects, since many of my students spend hours watching television or at babysitters' homes.

Students were highly motivated by the opportunity to present their completed projects. Some children needed 30 minutes to explain or read their work and answer questions. As the children showed or read their work, I learned, too. To my surprise, their enthusiasm and projects surpassed my expectations. One such example was Shannon's "Flying Machine Album."

"I wrote this one for you, teacher, and you're gonna love it!" He proudly held up his album and displayed each airplane picture and the accompanying descriptive sentence. He turned the album in my direction so I could see the special page of one jet refueling another in midair. "A gas station in the sky," he read, beaming at me.

After all the children had shared one or two of their projects, the projects were put on display, captioned with the children's names. All of a sudden there was not enough bulletin-board space. Teacher-made or commercial visual aids were removed or even covered by student projects. Older brothers and sisters began to pop in to see their younger siblings' work on display. My students loved seeing their first and last names printed boldly next to their productions. Occasionally I would see children tracing over their names as they stood next to a display. "I didn't know that I'd be famous," reported Becky as she followed each letter of her name with her finger.

Other exciting things happen with student writing, too. One day, Taylor, a shy little blond fellow, brought in a large white plastic bag. Inside was a huge sheet of heavy white paper. Proudly and secretively, Taylor sat on the little orange chair in front of his 20 classmates, who were sitting crosslegged on the red rug.

"I have a real treat for you all today. I wrote a poem!"

Taylor read his poem, obviously enjoying himself. When he was finished the children clapped loudly.

"I'll bet you guys didn't even know I was good at poems!"

The children certainly were impressed, and so was I. Months later, while the students were working on a sea-life unit, in came Taylor with another large white bag.

"Taylor's got a poem! Taylor's got a poem! Taylor's got a poem!" chanted Maura.

Taylor wouldn't acknowledge her statement. He just smiled as he once again took his place in front of the inquisitive group.

"You all remember my other poem about being in a plane? Well here's my new one. My mom helped me because she bought the paper and then she had to find this baby picture of me. I was only 2 years old and I was at the beach. Now, get ready, 'cause this poem really happened."

In the Sand

By Taylor

> When I was two I went to the beach. I put sand in my shoes. And in my diaper, too. The ocean made my cry. I was afraid of it. I thought I would die. But would I spit?

(After reading his poem, Taylor explained that he had sand in his mouth as well, so he needed to spit it out.)

Throughout the year students arrive at my classroom before 8 a.m. because they are anxious to share their stories. One day a parent arrived early with her son and asked if she could type her son's story, which had been recorded on tape. Her son, Claude, had made so many revisions the night before that he didn't get to bed until 10 o'clock and was unable to print the story in final form. I thanked the parent for her support and showed her where the primary typewriter was located. Claude's topic was one that was suggested in a study unit on wild animals.

The Ostrich Race

By Claude

> One day when I was running with an ostrich, my neighbor Maria said, "Are you crazy running with an ostrich? That's the fastest bird in the world!" I said, "Of course I am, why do you think I'm running with an ostrich!" Then I went past Jon's house. Jon said, "Are you crazy jogging with an ostrich, it's 10 past 9 o'clock." I said, "Of course I am." Then I went past Keith's house. He said, "Are you crazy jogging with an ostrich? You better get some sleep before you go jogging with an ostrich to school." The next day I went to school, jogging with my ostrich, and Mrs. Giordano said, "You brought a real ostrich to school!" And I said, "No that's just my dad!!!"

Claude read his story proudly. During the question period he explained how he had kept changing his story until he "liked it better." At the conclusion of his presentation, Claude announced: "Eye contact, please." (Claude was parroting my directions.) "If you want to tape a story and then have it typed my mom will type it. Remember, it's okay to keep changing you mind to make your story better."

Claude's mom, although much surprised, did finally consent to become a permanent fixture at the typewriter for the next month. And she was kept busy, too.

As you might guess, writing has assumed an increasingly important role in my classroom over the last dozen years. I once felt that it was difficult to fit writing into my schedule, but writing daily is now a priority.

The benefits of writing became evident to me as my students' writing experiences increased. Writing is individual, involving every child at his or her own level. Successes in writing have a domino effect, improving students' self-images as they write and share.

Writing also provides an avenue for the application of reading skills. After students have had opportunities to write their own stories, they gain a new respect for other authors and their works. Students also need to share what they have written, because it is through thinking, writing, reading, and listening that academic and personal growth take place. Furthermore, writing provides each student with a means of practicing and utilizing language. When a teacher wants to provide only the best learning for students, opportunities to write in a trusting atmosphere must be part of the daily program.

Writing in our classroom has been fun, both for the students and for me. I have worked hard to keep it that way. I learned long ago that student writing always needs to be supported and encouraged by positive comments made in an accepting manner by teacher and students alike. Publicly displaying student writing, talking about it, and presenting it to peers and parents provide opportunities for such positive reinforcement. This reinforcement serves as the key to the kind of classroom climate in which young children's writing can grow and flourish best. Creating such a climate is the first task--and maintaining that climate is a continuing challenge--for any teacher of beginning writers.

5. WRITING TO DEVELOP SELF-CONCEPT

By Barbara Brody Meyer

When teaching helps children strengthen their own views of self and develop good interpersonal skills, it can be an exciting challenge and a rewarding experience. Although I did not always consider these objectives to be part of my social studies curriculum, I now realize that developing a strong feeling of self is a first step in learning how to participate in groups, which is in itself a special goal of social studies teaching. The ability to communicate, the ability to work with others, and the ability to cooperate to solve problems are basic skills in a democracy. Only when students are involved in learning activities which take place in a positive classroom climate can the real learning of social studies occur.

Writing can play a crucial role in achieving this goal. If students write about themselves, they have the opportunity to discover their strengths and weaknesses, thus developing more accepting views of themselves and others. The writing ideas described here allow for self-discovery and emphasize the value of each individual child. When we carry out these ideas in class, students are not studying "about" social studies, they are involved in positive social interaction which produces more-meaningful and longer-lasting learning.

Elementary-grade students can engage in a wide variety of writing activities that develop positive self-concept. However, I have found two such activities especially useful: writing about a "special person of the week" and writing an autobiography. These activities can begin at any point during a school year and may be used over a large span of time, but they should not occur in isolation. When such activities are linked together and presented in a continuous manner, each activity is strengthened by the one that precedes it as well as by the one that follows.

The teacher's role is that of enabler and model. The teacher sets the stage by developing a classroom atmosphere that allows students to feel safe, to explore themselves, to open up and share with each other. The teacher shows, by example, ways to boost self-confidence, and the students copy this behavior in their own interactions. If the teacher stresses the value of each individual in a natural environment of caring, these lessons will not be gimmicks--and they will be successful.

Selecting different students as "special persons of the week" offers a fine opportunity not only to write but for students to be supportive of and to receive the support of their classmates. Each Friday we select a different child by randomly pulling an attendance card from a stack. This child becomes the "special person" for the following week. The weekend break allows time for the child to gather up items at home for the big week coming up. For the individual child and the entire group, this begins a rewarding set of learning activities.

First, the "special person" is given a bulletin board or area of the chalkboard on which to display photos, baby books, and other items that he or she wishes to share. In addition to those items brought to school from home, we display an instant photograph of the honoree, taken at school by the teacher. This important picture is mounted on colorful paper along with a piece of writing paper. Here the child writes information about himself or herself.

We undertake two writing activities each week. One is a class-dictated story that the teacher records on a large piece of paper. Students make up and share sentences about the special person. The statements must be positive in order to contribute to positive self-esteem. As they are voiced, the teacher records them for all to see. Many writing skills can be exercised in this group lesson as the children see their oral language take written form. The story is displayed for all to see during the week, but it goes home with the "special person." Many parents have remarked about the importance these stories have when they arrive home. They are taped on bedroom doors and often are displayed for months. These stories evidence the group's acceptance and appreciation of the individual.

Another writing activity is also carried out during the week. Students compile a book of stories, poems, puzzles, and illustrations about the "special person." The students share their contributions and then collect them into a booklet. On Friday the "special person" takes the booklet home to keep.

In addition to these writing activities, other things can be done to help children develop more positive images of themselves. For example, once each month I eat lunch with the "special persons" from the most recent weeks. We carry our lunch trays and bagged lunches back to our quiet classroom for a more personalized lunch period. Elementary school children enjoy this special attention, and the teacher can have some high-quality time with a few children. We all know how hard it is to find that time during the busy school day!

Special-person badges, hats and honors can also be used to give attention to the child as the student travels throughout the school building. Sharing time on Friday provides time for the honored child to demonstrate a special talent, skill, or interest.

All of these activities help me accomplish important social studies goals. Each of my classes enjoys the experience, and a "special feeling" develops as the year progresses. All children, regardless of intelligence, personality, or popularity, have the spotlight for a week, and in the process they develop increasingly good feelings about themselves.

Writing autobiographical accounts can also contribute to the development of positive student self-concepts.

> My favorite hobby is reading. What is yours? I like piano lessons. My favorite food is french fries. . . . One day I had a baby brother that was just born. I was jealous. I went upstairs and closed my door and cried.
>
> When my brother is 17 I am going to beat him up and put peanut butter on him and a hole gallon of milk on him and my cat is going to tell on me like he always does.

These excerpts from two second-grade student autobiographies derive their delightful honesty from shared emotions and humor. This type of writing happens when the children are given some direction.

First, I show the class how to create individual "me-mobiles." These mobiles are constructed from metal hangers, yarn, construction paper, white paper plates, and crayons. The students trace their own hands and cut out the letters of their names from the construction paper; the paper plates become their faces on the mobiles; and all are hung from the hangers with yarn.

Once this art project is well under way, we start our autobiographies. Half of the group retires to a private corner of the classroom to talk with the teacher about themselves, while the other students work on their "me-mobiles." Dividing the class into two smaller groups provides more opportunities for involving students in discussion. This serves as our prewriting activity. When the students eventually return to their desks to write, they have talked through some key ideas and have had a chance to ask questions. The small-group discussion also serves to motivate and build enthusiasm for writing about self.

Our discussions are always lively. We discuss such things as the students' hobbies, interests, pets, sports, vacations, and families. Invariably, sibling rivalry comes up, since young children are particularly interested in discussing this all-important part of their lives.

So that their autobiographies do not become dull recitations of facts, dates, and vital statistics, I introduce another element into the discussion: I share a humorous and true story from my own childhood. This helps build intimacy as I become someone "real" with a past that is rich in experience. By sharing myself I can reach out and develop trust with the students. This helps the new writers feel safe to be open and free in their own writing. My oral storytelling also gives the students a style to model when they write. No wonder the children leave the small group eager to write and tell the teacher about their feelings and experiences.

After children in the discussion group return to their desks to write, the remaining half of the class goes through the same process. After all writing is completed, students who wish to do so share their autobiographies.

My students seem to enjoy hearing their writings read aloud, and everyone gets to know each other a little better. The "me-mobiles" add an illustrative dimension to the experience. The entire activity, including the writing and artwork, can be completed in one or two class periods.

In addition to these major writing projects, writing can be used in other ways to foster the development of positive self-concepts in students. I have found the following four activities to be useful:

--Books about self: Throughout the year each student writes stories about different phases of his or her life. At the end of the year, these are collected in a folder or booklet so that each child has his or her own book about self.

--Measuring: Using rulers, yardsticks, and tape measures, the students measure various dimensions of their bodies--for example, circumference of head and length of arms and legs. These data can be charted, graphed, and written about from a variety of points of view.

--Journal writing: A daily period of time is set aside for free writing in personal journals. Although their contents are private, journals may include experiences that can be more fully developed later for a larger audience. This is one method that professional writers use which can be initiated by new writers. Writing for oneself is as satisfying as playing the piano for oneself, and introspective writing may be one of the students' more meaningful uses of writing throughout their lifetimes.

--Author badges: Badges can be used to encourage student writers. Naming student authors and praising their efforts serves to make the learning situation less intimidating. Teacher-made or student-made badges or tokens can be pinned to the students' clothes or stapled to their stories. These can be seen by others during the child's day, and the positive comments will be repeated.

Writing can be a very important tool of elementary school social studies teaching, especially when it focuses on student self-concept. The study of self gives students the opportunity to look at themselves and like what they see, an ability that is fundamental to healthy personality development. Writing can be used to probe, to record, and to communicate what we observe about ourselves. In fact, self-concept and writing are linked in several ways.

Writing not only expresses one's self, it is enhanced by one's concept of oneself. To write about any subject is to expose ourselves for others to see--our thoughts, our feelings, our knowledge, and our skills, to whatever degree they may be developed. It takes courage to do this. Having positive feelings about themselves encourages writers to be willing to share themselves with others through writing. Writing about themselves helps students develop this willingness.

Elementary school social studies can and should include time to focus on the individual. Doing so teaches appreciation for all members of the group. Self-concept writing clusters all these values and objectives together in a strong coalition of purpose.

One should undertake such classroom activities with considerable care and caution, however. Not all students feel free to share thoughts about themselves with others, and no one should ever be required to do so. Creating a classroom climate of trust, respect, and openness takes time. While writing, especially about one's self, can build such a climate, it also requires the existence of a supportive climate. The two develop hand in hand.

Furthermore, students need to focus on the positive in writing about themselves. They need to write about their likes, their hopes, the things they like to do or prefer, the attributes in themselves or others which they admire. "Me-mobiles," autobiographies, sentences, and stories about "special persons" should be positive statements if students are to feel free to explore themselves openly with their classmates.

Of course, primary-grade teachers may appear to have more time than other teachers to devote to self-concept writing. However, I have found that time devoted to such activities at any grade level is time well spent. The benefits are far-reaching, and they tend to humanize the classroom community. Using writing to accomplish basic social development can be an important aspect of elementary school social studies teaching and learning.

6. INTERVIEWING TO INITIATE WRITING

By Ada Marie Hooper

"Do you see other people in your family write?" I read aloud from the attitude survey. The five-year-old beamed as he replied: "Oh, yes. I see my mom write checks all the time."

After a survey of 63 kindergarten children, designed to measure their attitudes about composition, yielded only a few positive responses to the question about seeing grownups write, I had almost decided that writing by people other than students was nonexistent. Seldom did children in my class observe letter writing, journal writing, or any other kind of writing in their own homes. No wonder they didn't think much of writing when we mentioned or tried it in class!

Soon, I thought, this will change. We would have an opportunity for writing with a real purpose. The Gran Celebration was coming!

The "Gran Celebration," a tradition in the Wichita Public Schools, is a means of recognizing and honoring the senior citizens of the community. During this week-long event, grandparents and senior citizens visit classrooms throughout the school system to participate with the children in such activities as student-prepared luncheons, sharing of crafts and hobbies, and storytelling. The celebration had its beginning when a Wichita teacher, Connie Dietz, could not let the resources of a home for the elderly, located adjacent to her school, go untapped. She and her students "adopted" grandparents at the home. The experience was so worthwhile that the celebration idea was born. The continuing involvement of these individuals in our schools is a major benefit of the celebration. For my students, this event provides an unparallel opportunity to develop student readiness for writing.

Our Gran Celebration writing project consists essentially of two parts: information gathering and writing.

Gathering information about grandparents and older citizens of the community serves as our prewriting activity. The method we use to gather this information is the interview. Because many children in the particular area where I teach come from mobile families, the chance of a classroom visit from their grandparents may be remote, so we had to discover a way to bring them into the classroom vicariously. To capture some of the fun of learning about the "gran" citizens of our own families, as well as to gain an appreciation for these people, we devised a simple interview form that asks for such information as place of birth, where the grandparents had attended school and what it was like, early experiences in their lives, and what the grandparents considered to be the most important changes in the world during their lifetimes.

The first interviews conducted by my kindergarten classes five years ago met with amazing success. Every child brought some information from home. Many brought photos to accompany the completed interview sheets. Each year since then, working as a group, we formulate the questions for the interviews as we discuss that we would like to know that our grandparents could tell us. The only guideline is that the questions must not be the kind that can be answered with a "yes" or "no." Here is an opportunity to help children discover information about their own heritage as well as to observe writing being used as a vital tool of communication between home and school.

The class prepares the interview questions a week before the Gran Celebration begins. The day after the interview forms are sent home, children begin bringing the completed ones back to school. The results are immediately shared by reading them to the class and then summarized. Each student helps the teacher select the most interesting or vital parts of his or her interview, and these are typed on a primary typewriter. The summaries are then displayed on the celebration bulletin board. A border of colored balloons and curling paper streamers surrounds a display of photos and descriptions of very special people. By the end of the week, the contents of the bulletin board have overflowed onto the walls surrounding it, and almost every child has a bit of heritage displayed.

Some interviews are completed by the grandparents themselves. A note sent with the interview form asks that, if possible, the respondent read the questions and reply orally, then write out the responses on the form. Sometimes it is necessary for parents to complete the interview form, drawing on their own memories of their parents who may be either deceased or living some distance away. Some parents have helped arrange interviews via long-distance telephone--ironically, since the telephone is one of the technological inventions that have decreased our need to communicate through writing. At the insistence of their children, other parents have made special trips to neighboring towns to track down the sought-after knowledge.

Obviously, kindergarten children must rely to a large extent on the literate abilities of others to help them complete this project. The possibility that some children will not be helped with their interviews diminishes as parents or older siblings notice the bulletin board and read with interest the results of our interviews. Parents, just as children do, like to see their efforts displayed. If a child's family isn't represented on the board, other family members are motivated to help complete the interview.

Other teachers successfully use the interview technique with older classes, letting students devise their own questions and record the responses themselves. In some cases the interviews are not limited to family members but are open to any older persons in the neighborhood. Sharing the findings is as important as conducting the interviews. Students have made books about "gran" citizens for use in the school library, created displays showing the various occupations of older citizens over the past century, and labeled maps with places of birth, showing the rich and diverse makeup of the local community.

Many students involved in this activity bring real objects to school to show examples of special talents or interests of older citizens. Treasured relics from the past frequently appear. One year my students brought in so many items that the entire school was invited to come to our classroom to view the collection and hear the students tell about the objects. The items included a cylinder-type phonograph, metal containers for such things as talcum powder and cure-all ointment, kitchen gadgets that were popular decades ago, wearing apparel, writing instruments (few children had ever seen a fountain pen), old books, and--perhaps the most unusual item--a glass eye that had belonged to a great-grandparent. Each object had a history to be told and recorded.

Learning about our older citizens and paying sincere attention to a sometimes-neglected segment of society has created closer relationships in families and the school communities. Senior citizens, finding a warm welcome in classrooms, have begun volunteering their services in schools. Teachers, viewing these volunteers as a rich resource, are delighted with their talents and their dependability.

Aside from these important outcomes, perhaps the major value of incorporating Gran Celebration activities into the crowded curriculum is the opportunity for writing to take place for a real purpose. My kindergarten students are the bearers of important written messages as they carry home the interview forms. They observe parents and grandparents writing as they complete the interviews. These children develop a real understanding of the power of written symbols as they discover that interesting information can be preserved to be understood and repeated by someone in another place and time.

Summarizing--drawing from information those points deemed most important by the student--is a new concept for most five-year-olds. Because the summaries are transcribed from the students' own words, the information displayed on our classroom bulletin board now "belongs to" the students.

Weeks after the celebration, little stories often emerge in our "writing center" about favorite experiences that students have enjoyed with their grandparents or tales related to the children about grandparents or older citizens. Though these "stories" may look like a mass of squiggles, letter forms, and unknown symbols to the literate world, they are the beginning attempts of writers experimenting with written communication. My students now know that what is thought can be spoken and that what is spoken can be written. The only need for a five-year-old at this point is to have a willing adult nearby to hear the story as it is being "read" and transcribe it into conventional symbols that the rest of the world can understand.

For older students who have already learned to understand and use conventionalities to convey messages, the possibilities for writing are really sparked by the Gran Celebration. Again, the importance of writing for a real purpose is emphasized as youngsters create stories, both real and fantastic, which they share with real audiences either in their own classrooms, via the library (where library pockets and checkout cards are pasted into carefully made student books), or posted attractively on a hall bulletin board.

The memorabilia collected also spark stories. For example, "Grandma's Washboard," written in the first person, describes the weekly task of rubbing the farm clothes against the metal ridges of the washboard and the smell of lye soap produced by Grandma herself. Such writings may draw on imagination as well as on research; in order to make their stories authentic, students search the library for descriptions, directions for use, and other vital information about old artifacts.

Script writing finds its way into the classrooms as dialogue for puppets is set to paper. Letter writing, script writing, story writing, book writing--all the work of students, all with a purpose and audience--can be spurred by a simple interview focused on a different generation and a different world than now exists.

During the final month of school, when I again administer the survey of attitudes associated with composition, I get positive responses from my students. Not only have they seen grownups write things other than checks, they have played an important role in a writing project. They have seen adults writing as they filled out the interview forms and as their teacher transcribed oral ideas and reports. They have seen written products produced by other students of their school, and they have borrowed precious student-made books from the library. They have listened to the writing of other students as our entire class stops in the hall to hear the bulletin-board stories read aloud. My students have attempted stories of their own with the power and conviction that five-year-olds can bring to the task of writing. With pencils in hand, students "talk" their stories as the pencils make hieroglypics decipherable only to the authors.

By "getting into" writing in this way, these children may realize that they are on the verge of a great personal discovery--that very soon the pencils they hold will make meaningful marks that others can understand.

7. DEVELOPING WRITING READINESS IN YOUNG CHILDREN

By Mary McFarland

Kindergarten and first-grade teachers the world over affirm that their young students are (1) curious and eager to learn, (2) fascinated by pictures--especially large, brightly colored pictures--and (3) pleased when they recognize that they are beginning to do what older learners do (learn new words, "read," "write," think and talk about the real world). Primary-grade teachers can capitalize on these special and delightful characteristics in the process of developing writing readiness in their young students as they deal with social studies subjects. Such teaching can be built around a social studies study print or other large picture related to social studies. The children can study and discuss the print, making observations and recognizing new words associated with reality. They can then see their own thoughts in written form as they dictate a story based on the picture which the teacher can print on the board. Follow-up activities can provide additional oral language experience and vocabulary development linked to social studies. Such an approach goes far toward providing "direct and specific instruction" for young children which promotes the basics of thinking, reading, and writing in the content area of social studies.[1]

A lesson such as the one described in this chapter essentially involves four phases: (1) prewriting (discussion of the picture), (2) oral storytelling (children dictate as teacher records story on the board), (3) seatwork (done by children after story is written), and (4) in-school and home (optional) followup. The remainder of this chapter presents step-by-step instructions for conducting the lesson, along with brief suggestions for preparation and followup.

The sample activities included in this article are from a Title IV-B project, Discussion and Story Writing in Primary Social Studies, implemented by kindergarten and first-grade teachers in the Parkway School District, St. Louis County, Missouri.

Selecting a Picture

The first task for the teacher is selecting an appropriate picture. Several commercially published sets of social studies study prints are available, or any picture can be used if it is large enough to be seen by all of the children, if it has sufficient detail to elicit many different comments from the children, and if it is reality-based in content, so as to draw out the special reality-based vocabulary associated with social studies and expository or factual writing. Colorful pictures in social studies texts may be used if they meet these criteria and are related to the students' experience.

Developing a Lesson Plan

The lesson plan should be built around specific questions designed to stimulate student comprehension and idea-making. Many questioning strategies exist for helping youngsters make sense of pictures and for helping them invent meaningful ideas about what they see. One such set of questions is built around three levels:

1. Factual/literal--What can be seen in the picture?
2. Comprehension/interpretation--What is happening in the picture?
3. Evaluation/application--What are the relationships between this picture and other things you have experienced? What do you think or feel about what is shown in the picture?

Specific questions developed at these three levels are included in the sample lesson plan that follows. These questions should be used merely as a guide; they need not necessarily be asked in the order originally devised, nor do all of them need to be asked. Many additional questions will undoubtedly come to mind in response to ideas volunteered by the children as the lesson progresses.

Conducting the Lesson

Step 1: Prewriting. Display the picture (of a Japanese family eating a meal) and explain, "We are going to talk about living in Japan." Read the following text to the class:

> This family lives in the biggest city in the world. The city is Tokyo, in the beautiful country of Japan.
>
> Mr. Okamatsu works for a busy newspaper in the city. He takes many of the pictures that are printed in the

newspaper. When Mr. Okamatsu comes home at night, the whole family bows politely to welcome him. Then he changes from his suit into a loose robe called a kimono. Mrs. Okamatsu helps him put on his kimono, and the children bring him his slippers.

Mrs. Okamatsu made a good dinner of fish, vegetables, rice, and tea. The Okamatsus have rice at every meal, like most families in Japan. Mimi helped her mother cook the food and set the table.

Now Mother and Father, Grandmother and the children are sitting on cushions around a low table, eating their good dinner. Japanese families do not use knives and forks. They like to eat with chopsticks.

The floor of the Okamatsu house is covered with soft, springy straw mats, called tatami. Mother is proud of her clean mats. She brushes them until every speck of dust is gone.

The walls of the rooms are made of paper. They slide open and shut. The children can easily take them down to make one big room. They can slide open part of the wall to make a door. Everyone has to move carefully in a Japanese house, or he might tear holes in the paper walls.*

Lead the discussion by asking children questions at three levels of difficulty.

Level 1: Literal/factual

--How many people are there?

--How many adults are there?

--How many children are there?

--What are they eating?

--What are they sitting on?

Level 2: Comprehension/interpretation

--What is happening in the picture?

--What do you notice about the clothes?

--What do you notice about the way they are eating?

--What meal do you think this is? Why?

--Who do you think the people at the table are?

---

*Reprinted by permission from Families Around the World: Living In Japan, teacher's manual, by Patricia Stoddard. Copyright 1966 by Silver Burdett Company.

Level 3: Evaluation/application

--How are their cups different from ours?

--What do they sit on? (Pillows on the floor.) What does this mean about the table? (It would have to be low.)

--How would you feel sitting on the floor?

--How is this family (different from/like) American families?

Step 2: Writing (telling) the story. Ask the children to suggest a title for the story. Encourage them to select a broad title. The following comments may help the students develop their story.

Beginning of story:

--How do you want to get started?

--What do you want to talk about first?

Main part of story:

--What else do you see in the picture?

--What might be in that scene that does not show in the picture?

--What kind of person is (each family member)? What is that person like?

--What would (he/she) do or say if (present some hypothetical situations)?

End of story:

--What do you want to say to finish this?

--How does the story end?

As the students develop their ideas, record as many details as possible on the chalkboard. When they decide that they have finished, read the "story" back to them, making sure that you have noted all the important points. (As soon as possible after class, type a more-polished draft of the story, fleshing it out with any details that you didn't have time to record. Use a primary typewriter and then make copies for all the students, to be passed out the following day.)

Step 3: Seatwork. Point to some of the key words in the story and ask each child to pick one word and make a picture about it. (Some key words might be chopsticks, tatami, kimono, city.) As the children finish their pictures, call them up to your desk one at a time and ask each child to make up a title for his or her picture and make up one sentence that tells about the picture. Using a primary typewriter, type the title and the sentence as the child watches. Then ask the child to read aloud the title and the sentence. (Depending on their reading abilities, some children may need to rely on their memories.) This step is important, because it helps young children learn that their thoughts can be written down on paper in words that can be read by other people.

Step 4: Followup. Pass out copies of the typed story and ask the class to "read" it aloud together. Then let individual children take turns "reading" their sentences and telling about their pictures. Encourage the children to take home their pictures and stories and "read" them with their parents.

Evaluating the Progress of the Class

In order to determine whether students are making progress in developing coherent stories and in using language that corresponds to specific pictorial examples of experience, teachers should periodically evaluate the picture-story lessons they conduct. This can be accomplished by videotaping and then reviewing a lesson, by having a colleague observe the lesson as it progresses, or by reflecting on what happened in the lesson when time is available to do so. Regardless of which approach is used, certain criteria need to be considered.

The matrix in Figure 3 offers useful guidelines for evaluating the quality of student discussion and stories generated by lessons based on the model described above. Keep in mind, however, that an achievement level of only 3 or 4 may be a reasonable expectation for young children, since the purpose of the activity is to provide opportunities for children to begin to practice discussion and to follow the logical development of a story in a pressure-free, risk-free environment. The evaluative criteria merely set forth for the teacher some reasonable and possible outcmes.

Teachers who use this approach to introduce writing in primary-grade social studies find that their students grow in the abilities to discuss reality-based topics and to dictate stories about these topics which are characterized by increasingly greater coherence. Such lessons represent deliberate instruction designed to provide foundations of expository writing in elementary social studies.

Figure 3

CLASS EVALUATION CRITERIA

Criteria for Evaluating Class Discussions

Key: 1 = all children all the time
2 = most (3/4) children most (3/4) of the time
3 = many (1/2) children much (1/2) of the time
4 = some (1/4) children some (1/4) of the time
5 = few or no children seldom or never

Criteria	Performance Levels	
Contributes ideas during lesson	______	
*grasps main ideas		______
*stays on topic		______
Uses simple sentences and appropriate English	______	
*uses "reality" vocabulary		______
*uses "social studies" vocabulary		______
Listens attentively	______	
*reacts to ideas expressed		______
*appears to comprehend		______
"Reads" story aloud when complete	______	
Average	______	

Criteria for Evaluating Stories

Key: 1 = outstanding (true for entire story)
2 = above average (true for 3/4 of story)
3 = adequate (true for 1/2 of story)
4 = below average (true for 1/4 of story)
5 = poor (true for very little or none of story)

Criteria	Performance Levels	
Relevance/coherence	______	
*ideas are related to topic		______
*ideas are related to one another		______
Organization	______	
*story has topic (main idea) sentence		______
*story has detailed sentences		______
*story has concluding sentence		______
Development	______	
*sentences describe reality		______
*concepts are related to social studies		______
*vocabulary is related to social studies		______
Average	______	

Notes

1. Barry K. Beyer, *Back-to-Basics in Social Studies* (Boulder, Colo.: Social Science Education Consortium, 1977).

8. EXPLORING THE PAST: WRITING ABOUT REAL STUFF

By Kristin Smyka

Our first-grade class journeyed into the past one day when I transformed the classroom into an old "attic." I arrived at school in old-fashioned garb that I had accumulated from auctions, rummage sales, and the closets of indulgent friends. Student enthusiasm was noticeably high, and I was greeted with a barrage of morning quips ("Hey, teacher, it's not Halloween today") while variations of "Ms. Smyka, you look pretty" filled the classroom as the children tugged at and unabashedly examined my clothing.

I wanted to involve my class in writing that would intrigue them while simultaneously promoting other skills. Young children commonly use the past tense in their writing, so a historical context seemed a natural choice for this lesson. To accomplish my writing goals, I knew that I would have to develop a series of activities that integrated all the senses and included a variety of prewriting experiences. I would need to prepare concrete examples. These conditions would provide a useful context for the writing we would do.

My six-year-olds clustered around me as we gathered to begin our day. First I explained that we were going to think about a long time ago. We would do things to help us see, feel, hear, smell, and talk about a different way of living.

I asked each child to find a quiet, private place in the classroom. Some children curled up under tables; others stretched in more-obscure corners, clutching pillows or with cherished toys in tow. I turned the lights off and we listened to a recorded version of the song "Today, Yesterday, Tomorrow."* I played the song twice so that children could listen to the lyrics.

---

*From the album Imagination and Me (Custom Records Production, St. Louis, Missouri).

We regrouped on our carpet and discussed the notion of time. J.C. commented that "there's different kinds of time" and that "some are gone." John observed that he hadn't always had his Tigey and Tigey, Jr., but that he would "keep them for lots of tomorrows."

We also briefly role-played some situations in order to help clarify simple time distinctions. Julie dramatized her play activities of "yesterday," as a two-year-old toddler, and today, as a first-grade student. We talked about how "yesterday" can mean more than "the day before." We distinguished between the past and current events, recognized as "now" or "today." Kirsten thought that "we change when time goes by." John wasn't sure whether Tigey and Tigey, Jr. would change, but he did acknowledge that his beloved stuffed animals were "starting to go old."

I had moved out most of our classroom chairs and tables the evening before. I hung crepe paper and explained that it represented cobwebs. I carried in an old chair, a fan, a box of books, and an antique trunk stuffed with old-fashioned paraphernalia. This was the "attic" we were about to explore.

After the children paired up with partners, each team came to the trunk and selected an item while other children walked through the cobwebs and examined the other attic furnishings. When all the teams had objects from the trunk, they spent a few minutes sharing their ideas about how they might have been used.

We reconvened as a large group and talked about how the children had felt when they looked into the trunk or reached in to take an article. I asked questions about smell, sight, touch, and sound. Soon we had a list of collectively descriptive words, which I recorded on a large sheet of paper visible to everyone. The words ranged from "squirmy," "tingly," and "breath-holding" to "icky," "yucky," and "aargh." I pointed out that some words described people's feelings, while others identified smell, touch, or appearance. Deanne reported that her grandmother had a trunk filled with "old stuff she loves and keeps." Connie said that her mom "doesn't want old junk."

The teams rejoined, and each pair chose a place in the room where the partners could talk with one another. I had typed some questions and run off copies for everyone. The children read the questions silently while I read aloud: "What do you think the object is? When do you think it was made? How do you think it was used? Who do you think owned it? Do you think this could be used today? If so, in what manner? Why was it in the trunk? Who do you think put it in the trunk?"

The room exploded with chatter as teams discussed new ideas in response to the questions. The children were eager to share their theories, so we reassembled as a large group and the students described their hypotheses.

Linda and Shaun related a long story about "these two kids who got some pennies from their parents and went to the story and bought this bottle of medicine for their sick uncle, and brought it home and smelled it and almost threw up because it was so rotten. They threw it out in the barn and some other kid found it years later and washed it out and kept it because it was such a beautiful blue bottle." Other versions--equally rambling but predictably fascinating--were volunteered.

Up to this point the children had been using numerous skills. Verbal expression, storytelling, conversing, imaging, decision making, creating, and sharing--all seemed to be flourishing. Equally apparent was every child's active participation in the prewriting process. Now we were ready to transfer that rich, vibrant, kinesthetic talk to paper.

Students picked up paper and pencils and moved to areas where they could write privately and comfortably. We closed our eyes and "made movies in our heads." I talked through the simulated attic trip, cueing children with words from our group list. We recalled class members' descriptions of smells and feelings. I reminded the children of the hypotheses that were suggested during the group discussion. I asked the children to make up "movies" about their old objects and write them down.

I circulated to offer spelling assistance. When a child asked, "How do you spell. . . ?" I said the letters as I wrote the word, providing a model for the writer who then copied it onto his or her paper. Kids wrote, erased, crossed out, erased, taped ripped papers, and kept on creating for a solid half-hour. We stretched, did some deep breathing, and then rejoined partners to exchange stories.

Sharing is an important part of the writing process. Each child read his or her completed writing to a partner. I asked each student to say one good thing about the other person's paper. Our room filled with "warm fuzzies" as listeners reacted to writers with such feedback as "I liked how you told about the boy in the picture" and "You used a lot of good words in your story."

Then we formed a large group, and some children volunteered to read their stories aloud. We listened, laughed, and offered more responses, such as "I never thought of that" and "Good idea, partner!"

Finally, to conclude our morning, we listened to the song again. It was a nice way to summarize our work. It helped slide us into the routine of "today," so lunch became a joyous prospect.

Later that afternoon, the stories were laboriously recopied. I burned the edges of the finished papers so they would look old and weathered. The children assisted, then mounted their stories for display on the hallway bulletin board.

The major goal of this lesson was to allow my students to get better acquainted with writing. They were involved in each of the basic stages of the writing process--prewriting, composing, and rewriting--in a way that made writing fun and relatively easy for them.

Beginning writers cannot be expected to express themselves well without concrete experiences to which to refer. In order to help students write, teachers need to provide situations in which a young child is able to assume the role of writer, address a specific audience, use a particular format, and consistently use time or tense.

Developmentally, six-year-old children are egocentric. They perceive the world from their own personal points of view, and each child is the core of his or her world. Ultimately, writing will reflect a child's ability to perceive situations from varying perspectives; first-graders, however, tend to react to occurrences from the standpoint of "me, myself, and I." This is a delightful and natural point of view, so little people can be directed to explore the phenomenon of self from expressive classroom activities.

Young children also need to participate actively in the writing process. A classroom situation provides an accessible and nonthreatening environment for individual, team, and large-group exploration. Children experience learning in a variety of forms. Music, language, listening, and rhythm are all infused into one experience. Discussion clarifies thinking, exposes the child to diverse points of view, and promotes collective interaction. Kinesthetic participation can be a powerful strategy when teachers engineer situations in which students draw on all their senses to process information.

Thus writing, for the beginning writer, takes a lot of beginning. When children have something to say or express, the writing process can be enriched by situations that give them prewriting confidence. Writing can also be facilitated by providing a meaningful purpose or context. In the lesson described here, students wrote answers to questions about the objects they had selected. However, other tasks might have been just as appropriate. The following variations on the task could also be tried with students:

--Shift roles, while writing, and imagine that you are the person in an old picture. Write about where you were when the photograph was taken.

--Imagine that you are the old spoon in the trunk. Write about three of the people who used you. Explain how you ended up in the trunk.

--Using a book that illustrates a historical happening, describe one of the illustrations by writing about the colors, artistic media, special features of the illustration, and so on.

--Pretend that you are a creature from history. (We studied dinosaurs, and children selected pterodactyl, stegosaurus, tyrannosaurus Rex, etc.) Someone will ask you questions about your life, (What do you eat? Where do you live?) Write the answers.

--Read aloud the clues from the preceding activity. Let the students guess, in writing, the identity of each "mystery history character."

--Listen to a reading of an old newspaper clipping. Then rewrite the situation, substituting details that would be plausible today.

--Identify historical references encountered every day (in advertisements, clothing displays, restaurant decor, etc.) and write about the "oldness" in a "now" environment.

--Put on different old hats and imagine that you are living in a past time. Write about the person who would probably wear that kind of headgear.

--Find an old shoe. Write about where it has been and whose feet have been inside it.

--Pretend that you live in 1881. Write about your thoughts as you bury a message for someone to find 100 years later. Write the message.

Support is also essential for youngsters when they begin to write. In this lesson we supported each other's perceptions by verbal collaboration (partner dialogue) and positive reinforcement ("Say one good thing about your partner's paper").

I display the children's written work because youngsters need to see, literally, that writing is talk written down. Finally, I encourage them to give the gift of self by sharing their creations and recognizing the value in a peer's creation.

9. BRAINSTORMING AS A PREWRITING ACTIVITY

By Virginia Pfotenhauer

Research suggests that an important variable affecting the quality of student writing is the amount of time devoted to prewriting activities.[1] These activities are crucial because they help students solve the perplexing (for them) problem of what to do once they have been given a writing assignment. For, our assumptions to the contrary, good student writing does not begin with an assignment. It begins when students have something of their own to say. And helping them discover this something is the prime focus of any prewriting activity.

Useful prewriting activities come in many forms, but probably one of the most useful is brainstorming. At times an unrestricted, almost free-association type of search for a topic, brainstorming can also be a deliberate way of evoking students' reactions to or ideas about a subject. Brainstorming can be used to elicit reactions to reading, pictures, or field trips. Whatever form it takes, it serves as a catalyst for helping students find something worthwhile to write about.

Brainstorming is not difficult to do. For a teacher, the strategy essentially involves stimulating students to think about an old topic in new ways. For example, consider a recent classroom dialogue in which my fifth-graders and I were brainstorming, trying to discover a topic that interested them--one that would tap <u>their</u> resources rather than mine or those of some outside authority. We had begun with "favorite places," moved to "admired people in American history," and finally settled on objects or possessions important to us and admired by others.

I knew at the time that I was working with an intelligent group of 10- and 11-year-olds, but what I had not accurately assessed was their level of sophistication. I was in for a big surprise and an interesting revelation. It was not long before I discovered that these youngsters understood the meaning of the term "status symbol."

Our prewriting discussion was focused on valued possessions. I asked "What is a status symbol?," expecting wide-eyed stares and silence.

From the far corner: "Well, something you have and prize that makes you feel important."

Other definitions were fast in coming.

"Few others have it. Something different. It attracts attention."

"I know a kid who has arthritis, and that's unusual for a kid. . . ."

"But nobody wants that!"

"It's something someone has that others might want, too. But not many can have the same thing. It's too expensive or too hard to get."

Since it was apparent that we wouldn't be able to agree on one definition, we tried for some examples. We would have to fully understand the concept before we could write about it.

"What are some possessions or objects people your age--or younger--might consider status symbols?" I asked.

"For kids younger than us they might be some of those toys you see on television--a Big Wheel or a five-speed bike."

"Or owning a 'Star Wars' lunchbox . . . or if a kid can swim or dive."

"For kids our age it might be having a minibike--not just a ten-speed 'regular' bike because they're getting common."

"Having your own phone number listed in the book after your parents' number."

"Candy underwear! They have it for kids and grownups. My grandpa sells it."

"Playing in a rock band."

"Owning a football autographed by a famous player like O.J. Simpson or Joe Namath."

"Taking private tennis lessons in a building somewhere, not in a city park. And not in a group, either."

We decided to pursue the discussion. We had everyone's attention.

"How about teenagers? What are their status symbols?" I asked next.

"Levis or pants with a special name on the back pocket, like 'Calvin Klein.'"

"Real leather jackets."

"Oh, those are fads, not status symbols," someone objected. "Fads change faster and go out of style."

"It's more like having your own car."

"Or your own telephone . . . or checking account."

"Having an expensive stereo set."

"Or owning an electric guitar."

"Or getting your driver's license before any of your friends do."

The children were much more knowledgeable than I had thought!

"What about college students? What do you see as their status symbols?"

"Driving a Corvette. Or maybe a souped-up Trans Am."

"Having their own apartments."

"Going skiing or hunting out West. And wearing one of those baseball caps with a visor that says 'Purina.'"

"Owning a customized van with stereo music, a sink, curtains, and carpeting all over the floor and walls. And maybe there's a picture of a sunrise in pink and orange painted on the side."

This was worth pursuing. Now we moved to adults.

"What about adults? Do adults have their own status symbols?"

"Oh yes." There was much nodding of heads. "Even more than teens or kids."

"Such as?" I asked.

"Well, it used to be big shiny cars with lots of chrome, pushbuttons, and all those gadgets, the kind that practically took two parking spaces. But now it's a little shiny car with some of those same gadgets, but that gets more mileage than your neighbor's car."

"Having a live-in maid like at the governor's mansion. Wow! That would be neat."

"Owning a great big diamond ring."

"Taking a trip to Africa and going on a safari. Or taking a cruise in winter on one of those great big ships with swimming pools, dining rooms, and decks."

"Having the same license number as your address. Or having a low-numbered license number--although my dad says that isn't hard to get."

"Or having something on your car license <u>instead</u> of a number. I saw this car on my vacation last summer, and all it said was 'Pablo.' No number at all."

"Owning a fancy fur coat, like mink, for those who don't mind wearing an animal. Or having a big, fancy house high on a hill, looking down."

"Owning a condominium in Florida that you only use certain months of the year."

"Having membership in a tennis or country club."

"Having a dog so special that he drinks only distilled water. I read about a dog like that who's on television."

By now, we had just about exhausted our supply of answers. The students had been most interested, and it seemed that we would have something to write about. Then one more question came to mind.

"Can owning a status symbol make you happy?" I asked.

Thoughtful expressions appeared. There was some nodding, some dissent.

"Well, I suppose so. It might make you feel important."

"I suppose for a while it could, until you outgrew it. Then maybe you'd want something else."

"Depends. Depends upon <u>why</u> you wanted it."

"I'd take a minibike any day."

Then, from the back of the room, came this contribution:

"You know, I was just thinking. All the status symbols we've mentioned so far cost money. Well, I have an uncle who travels all over the United States on his bicycle with his dog. He's even had his picture taken and there was an article about him in a paper. People have gotten to know him. He doesn't own much, and he takes everything he needs right with him wrapped up on that bicycle. He writes stories and poems, but he doesn't have a regular job. He's against pollution and all the lies of advertising, so he doesn't take any work connected with that. He leads a very simple life, and he doesn't envy the things other people own. And I think that for him, living without a lot of things and doing pretty well without them is a status symbol."

Silence. Then heads nodded. The student's observations had been understood, accepted. The discussion had ranged from diamond rings to fancy houses to an almost complete lack of worldly possessions. Each might be a status symbol to someone.

"Can we write about this?" I asked. "Could we put it down on paper for someone to read?"

We had found a topic. Ideas had been generated. For all of us it was an interesting topic. The students began to pick up their pencils, having a sense of what they were thinking and beginning to get it laid out. They could forget word choice and spelling right now. The job involved just getting the general ideas into words and onto paper. Later there would be fleshing out of ideas, expanding, arranging, eliminating, narrowing of the topic. Because individuals write differently and better when they write for an audience--a built-in motivator--I asked the children to keep in mind for whom they were writing.

Later, during the rewrite stage--because good ideas need correct spelling and punctuation as well as special attention to word choice--students would work on clear, crisp diction; they would develop the details and attempt to say ordinary things in extraordinary ways. They would "polish until it shines" and think of titles that would "grab" a reader.

For some youngsters writing is painful, perhaps because it is personal and individualistic. For others it is difficult because it is hard to put into writing what one thinks. For all students, writing may be a real chore simply because it is often hard to get started. Brainstorming is one effective way to get started--to think up a topic, to zero in on it from many different perspectives as illustrated here, and to think of something to say about it. Prewriting helps students accomplish these three goals, and brainstorming is one of the most useful of all prewriting activities.

Notes

1. Elizabeth F. Haynes, "Using Research in Preparing to Teach Writing," English Journal, January 1978, pp. 82-88.

10. USING A WORD CACHE TO DEVELOP VOCABULARY

By Beverly Chadburn

The film about Chief Joseph was well done. It tied in exactly with the Indian unit, a subject with which the kids were really involved. The class was enthusiastic, full of ideas, new information, and insights. It was time for these students to put down some of their learning and feelings on paper.

The announcement of a writing assignment frequently resembles a death knell. Enthusiasm suddenly seems drained from students who moments before had been bursting with energy. Often, their main response to such an assignment is to squirm with frustration. Blank expressions spread over faces; blank papers stare back from desk tops. What has happened to these youngsters? How can their mood change so quickly? What have I done wrong?

Teachers, administrators, and, most important, the frustrated students in such a setting all need to realize that, up to a point, nothing is wrong. The problem is that an important part of the teaching process needs to be expanded. Something has been left out. But what is the vital omission? Students have no idea what has caused the breakdown in their interest except that they "cannot think of anything to write." Teachers, too, may be at a loss to explain why an exciting lesson has come suddenly to a halt. Moreover, even if they have a clue to the reason, they are not sure of the remedy.

In many cases the trouble stems from lack of ability on the part of students to put together all of the tasks which are required to write even a single sentence: choosing a topic, narrowing or broadening that topic, giving accurate and interesting information about the topic. What are some special descriptive words to electrify a "blah" statement? How are such words spelled and put together to make a readable sentence? Clouding all these issues is the nagging suspicion of most youngsters in school that they do not have the ability to perform the functions that writing demands.

Jim Sabol of Seattle Pacific University presents in his writing workshops some methods to stimulate the development of creative writing skills and help people put their ideas into self-satisfying, even exciting, writing.[1] His methods work well in social studies. One of the prewriting activities he recommends is designed to get kids ready to write and to help them feel confident that they can write. In the beginning it is highly teacher directed, with much class participation.

If a class has been studying a unit on Indians of the western half of the United States, for example, how many tribes can the students name? As the class thinks about possible answers, the teacher posts a large piece of butcher paper on the wall. (Recording the list on butcher paper, instead of on the chalkboard, permits the teacher to preserve the list for use on subsequent days.) At the top of the paper, on the left side, the teacher writes the word "naming" as the heading for a column. Under this heading, the teacher lists the names suggested by the students. Any name that is a correct response to the question should be written down; value judgments should be kept to a minimum. This process has two immediate benefits: (1) the students have some concrete terms to think about and (2) the knowledge that they can check the list for the correct spelling of a name or term will give the students confidence in using the terms in their writing.

After a good list of names has been developed, a second column of terms can be started. This column will record "attributing" terms. (It is a good idea to use a different-color marking pen for each column.) For example, the words "tall" and "extinct" might be attributing terms for a certain Indian tribe. Any word that refers to a distinctive feature of any of the terms in the naming column can be added to this list. The students should suggest at least one adjective for each term in the first column. Since an attributing word might apply to several terms in the naming column, and vice versa, it will not be feasible to print each attributing word across from the name it describes. However, the students can develop their own lists of names and matching attributing words.

When both columns are full, the students will have developed a word bank, or cache. ("Cache" is the term that was used by French trappers to refer to the storehouses of provisions which they hid in hollow trees or caves, to be revisited when they needed to replenish their supplies.) This word cache can be left posted on the wall for reference during the writing process.

The word cache can be expanded by adding a column of "predicating" or "doing" words--active verb phrases. For a unit on Indians in the western United States, this list might contain such phrases as "fought General Custer," "lived in the Great Basin," "found new animals to hunt," "fished for salmon," and "traded blankets." A fourth column might be devoted to "renaming" words--nouns or specific phrases that can be used as appositives to words in the naming column. The renaming column might include the names of individuals--for example, Crazy Horse and Sitting Bull--in addition to tribal subdivisions and terms related to roles and relationships.

The expanded word cache can be used as the basis for a composing activity in which each student writes one sentence, using as many words from the cache as can be appropriately put together. For example, a sentence about the Paiute Indians might read: "The poor, simple, wandering, hungry (all attributing words) Paiute (naming word) Indians (renaming word) lived in the Great Basin (predicating phrase), found few animals to hunt (predicating phrase), and could not farm (predicating phrase) the dry land."

The whole class might work cooperatively to compose a paragraph, given an initial topic sentence; for example, "The Indians of the California-Intermountain area had a variety of life styles." A sentence about each tribe of the region could then be compiled from the word cache, creating a paragraph full of descriptive words and information. This paragraph should be recorded on butcher paper and posted. Underlining the words taken from the cache helps students understand how they can use a word cache in their individual writing activities.

Word-cache lists can be made collectively by the whole class or by assigning small groups or individual students to compile the various columns. Once the students understand this process, they can work independently to make their own word caches as a prelude to individual writing projects. Going over these individual lists with students is an effective strategy for reviewing content as well as for checking on each student's progress.

Word caches are also useful for other kinds of writing; for example, blank verse or rhymed poetry. One pattern for writing blank verse is to start with a naming word, follow it with three attributing words, and end with a predicating phrase. Using this model, a fourth-grade student created these poems:

The Sioux:
organizing,
planning,
striking,
fought and died at Little Big Horn.

Nez Perce:
friendly,
gentle,
peace loving,
chased to extinction at Canada's border.

The Clatsop:
building,
hunting,
fishing,
vanished forever at the Pacific's edge.

A word cache can also be used to "take apart" a poem. As the poem is read, the students list names, words, and phrases in the appropriate columns of a word cache. In addition to serving as an exercise in literary composition, this process helps students understand the message and meaning of the poem.

All word caches should be saved for future reference in recall and review sessions or for incorporation into subsequent teaching units. If there is not sufficient wall space to leave them posted, the butcher paper can be rolled up and labeled by topic.

The word-cache method of stimulating thinking, organizing thought, and developing oral and written vocabulary is applicable to all grade levels, although the complexity of the writing activities will vary. The strategy works especially well in the social studies curriculum. The availability of a rich store of content-related words--all spelled correctly--will add variety and fluidity to students' writing, and teachers will begin to notice less resistance to writing assignments. No more squirming bodies and blank sheets of paper--students with access to a word cache are ready to write, and before long their papers will be filling up with words.

Notes

1. The word cache, or naming exercise, is the first of nine steps in a process taught by James Sobol, director of the Writing Northwest program at Seattle Pacific University.

III. USING WRITING TO LEARN SOCIAL STUDIES CONTENT

Through the use of social studies as a vehicle for learning how to write or for practicing writing, writing and social studies can complement each other in the elementary classroom. The use of writing as a tool for learning social studies content is another way in which writing and social studies can interact. In the former approach, learning how to write receives major emphasis, while social studies content serves primarily as a vehicle for such instruction. In the latter, learning social studies receives major attention while writing serves as a major vehicle or tool for accomplishing this learning. The ideas presented in the articles in this section stress ways of using writing to learn social studies content.

The first four chapters describe specific places in a social studies unit where writing can be used to help students learn social studies information or develop social studies generalizations. In all instances, writing is merely one--albeit an important one--of a number of techniques that can be woven together to achieve the subject-matter learning objectives of the unit. In each case writing is hooked to a commonly used classroom resource--visual aids, news media, library reference books--and to a particular social studies learning tool; for example, library research.

The authors of these articles are all experienced classroom teachers. In the first article, Ann Gibson describes a way to combine poetry writing with current events and local history. Bernice Crane, Dorothy Lamb, and Jackie Martin then explain a procedure that they use to help intermediate-grade students write original multiparagraph reports. Letter writing in current events serves as the subject of

Ellen Lazare Shatz's article, while Carol Palay describes how writing can be used to conduct simulated field trips in the social studies classroom. Whatever form the writing takes in each approach described here, the process by which it is produced remains essentially the same. Students engage in prewriting idea-generating, they compose a statement individually or with partners, and they share and revise what they have written. The outcome? Improved writing as well as new learning about a specific social studies topic!

The remaining three articles in this section explain in detail two different ways in which the systematic use of writing can be used as a vehicle for in-depth learning of social studies information and knowledge. Each author presents a step-by-step process whereby students use common social studies instructional materials in a writing task in order to accomplish substantive goals. In the process, these youngsters learn important skills. Betty Dyarmett shows how scriptwriting can be used to learn about the idea of democracy. Janet Cuenca's article describes how to help students construct a paragraph that includes only information which is relevant to the idea they wish to write about as they explore specific social studies topics. Jim Willcock explains a procedure for involving students personally in the subject they write about as a device for developing an empathetic understanding of social studies subjects. Each of these procedures may be used with a wide variety of social studies topics and subject matter and at a number of different grade levels.

The procedures and ideas presented here constitute only a few of the many ways in which writing and social studies content can come together in the elementary classroom. They illustrate how one can reinforce the other and how instruction in writing can be provided when it is important for students to write in order to achieve social studies learning goals. Such a combination of skill development and subject-matter learning may at first seem best suited only for intermediate-grade social studies and writing. However, the ideas presented here may actually be appropriate for social studies and writing instruction far beyond the elementary school classroom.

11. CURRENT EVENTS AND HISTORY THROUGH POETRY WRITING

By Ann Gibson

Can students learn about current events and history by writing poetry? That's exactly what has been happening in my classroom. My fourth-grade students write poetry in all areas of the social studies curriculum as a means of learning and understanding the information and generalizations we study. That the experience has been a rewarding one for the children is evidenced by an excerpt from a letter written by an "old" fourth-grader in May to be given to a "new" fourth-grader the following September:

> Wisconsin history can be fun, too. You will write a hole [sic] book. You will think you can't do it but you will do it a little bit at a time and pretty soon it will be all done and it will be a pretty good book.

The children in that fourth grade wrote numerous poems throughout the year. At the end of the year each child selected 26 of his or her own poems to be bound in an individual book--one poem for each letter of the alphabet. The technique used to write poetry for these books was the cinquain. Although a cinquain may take any one of several forms, the model we used is shown below:

noun
two describing words
three "ing" words
a four-word phrase
a synonym (for the noun)

Early in September, the class began to learn the form. They had class discussions on the nature and meaning of nouns, adjectives (describing words), phrases, and synonyms. Then they began to write cinquains as a group (usually on the chalkboard), using topics familiar to all the children. Among their tries were these:

recess
short, exciting
running, jumping, playing
a good time of day
fun

bus
big, yellow
bouncing, swaying, stopping
a noisy hot place
transportation

lasagne
thick, gooey
filling, nourishing, fattening
good to the last bite
lunch

Kurt
blond, athletic
learning, growing, playing
very good in math
golfer

Mimi
small, quick
smiling, running, asking
always cheerful and friendly
girl

After a few days, most children were feeling familiar enough with the form to write poems on their own. During their first efforts, they used a printed form with the following directions:

____
noun

________________ ________________
2 adjectives

________________ ________________ ________________
3 "ing" words

________________ ________________ ________________ ________________
a four-word phrase

____
a synonym (for noun)

Most of those poems were about pets, hobbies, family members, or neighborhood interests, for example:

Snoopy
tan, furry
digging, eating, sleeping
a very good pet
gerbil

Sandy
dirty, white
jumping, hiding, wetting
Tom's best friend
dog

Many of the students' cinquains were copied with marking pens on construction paper and displayed around the room and in the halls. Appreciative audiences did much to encourage further writing. Next year, our parents' club will type and assemble a literary magazine in order to provide our budding authors with a wider audience.

After writing about very familiar subjects, the children had had enough experience with the form to be comfortable with it, and they were able to concentrate on content. They began by writing about current events. They wrote about the election and the candidates. They wrote about a bad thunderstorm. During the crisis in Iran they wrote an abundance of poems. It was possible for them to express fears and concerns through their writing:

hostages
free Americans
waiting, praying, hoping
wanting to come home
prisoners

prisoners
men, women
eating, sleeping, waiting
all of them American
hostages

Every time there was a writing assignment, I provided time for each stage of the writing process--prewriting, writing, and editing. During the prewriting stage the class discussed the concepts they would be writing about, often listing vocabulary and sharing their own experiences with the subject. The writing stage (actually putting pencil to paper) often took less time that the prewriting stage, following it directly, a few hours later, or the next day.

The editing stage was done with a partner. After an author checked his or her own work, a friend checked to see whether the assignment had been followed correctly, looked for spelling or other mechanical errors, and read the poem for content. After peer editing, the work was handed to the teacher for comments or display. Teaching children to edit not only saved the teacher hours of correcting; more important, it taught the children to take responsibility for their own work instead of transferring that responsibility to the teacher.

While the children were writing and editing, I circulated among them to encourage ideas, admire work, and offer assistance. After a few weeks of practice, each child compiled 26 poems into a Wisconsin "ABC" book. Because Wisconsin history and geography occupy a large portion of the social studies program, this project combined those subjects with part of the language arts and handwriting curriculum.

Prewriting activities included checking out every alphabet book in the elementary school library and studying their texts, themes, and artwork. Following this, the class began a composite list of "Wisconsin words," beginning with Abe (a famous mascot of the Eagle Regiment during the Civil War), Appleton, and Aztalan and ending with zoo (the class had visited the Milwaukee zoo). They brainstormed and accepted any word anyone could justify as important to Wisconsin. They used their Wisconsin state history texts, maps, tourist brochures, and newspapers to find additional words.

When the class was ready to begin the actual writing process, they first selected a few letters that had many possibilities; for example, "T" (tobacco, tomahawk, telemark, Tomah, trees), "M" (Madison, mild, moraine, Marquette, Mendota, Muscoda), and "C" (cows, corn, cheese, canoe). Each day, two letter groups were "mined" for poem ideas. After a child had finished his or her cinquain, a friend would edit it for form, spelling, and content. The children became very careful about checking their own spelling before handing over their poems to friends. They also tried to say something specific in each poem and to avoid generalities. The only seriously overworked word was "big." When many "bigs" began appearing in poems, a class discussion was held in an attempt to find ways of handling this problem. Synonyms were offered, and children suggested other ways in which one might look at a subject without concentrating on size.

Once a poem had been edited, it was marked with the name of the author and the initials of the editor and given to the teacher. This identification gave the writer and editor a shared responsibility for the work. The teacher then gave the poem an "OK," made minor corrections, or wrote "See me" and returned it to the author. "See me" was used only when the poem needed major revision.

The author would then copy the poem on the bottom half of a sheet of paper, saving the top of the page for an illustration or a fancy rendering of the initial letter. Authors could illustrate their own poems or get help from friends. Some chose simply to design fancy letters for the top space and omit actual illustrations. A few of the resulting entries are reproduced below.

Abe	badger
feathery, brave	furry, brown
flying, seeing, screaming	running, eating, digging
mascot in the Civil War	Wisconsin's nickname
eagle	animal
heifer	Joliet
big, heavy	French, man
running, bucking, puffing	exploring, trading, canoeing
always very hungry	going down the river
cow	fur trader

When all the pages in each student's book of poems were complete and in order, two blank pages were added to the front of the book and one blank page was added to the end of the book for a title page and endpapers.

Care had been taken to leave a large margin on the left side of each page to provide room for binding. Each student collected pages A through M (including the two front blank pages) and sewed them together, using a strong embroidery needle and doubled, knotted thread (so that the needle would not slip off the thread). In the same manner, pages N through Z and the blank last page were sewn together. The two sections were then sewn together along the same line of stitches (using many of the same holes).

Once the booklet was sewn, the writer was given two six-by-nine-inch pieces of posterboard-weight cardboard and a piece of fabric and fabric-backed wallpaper for the cover. Several children made covers from the discarded legs of worn-out jeans. They removed the hems from the jeans, cut 11 inches of fabric from one leg, and trimmed away one seam. (The other seam was used for the spine of the book.) The process they used to put the complete book together is described in the accompanying box.

Directions for Binding "ABC" Books

Place the two pieces of cardboard on the wrong side of the fabric, leaving approximately ½-inch space between them (for the spine of the book). Glue the cardboard to the fabric, using white glue or dry mount from a photo-supply store. Let it dry thoroughly. Trim away excess fabric from the corners to reduce bulk. Turn the extra fabric over the cardboard and glue it down--sides first, then top and bottom. The cover is now ready for the pages.

Open the cover and glue the back of the last blank page to the inside of the back cover. The endpaper should cover the ragged edges of the cloth. Position the pages so that when the book is closed, the covers are even. Do this by closing the front cover and lining up the book. Do not glue the front cover to the front endpaper until it is even. Then glue the front cover cardboard to the first blank page. Weight the covers down until the glue is dry. The extra blank page at the front of the book is used as a title page.

Using a marking pen or stick-on letters, decorate the cover of the book with the title and the name of the author.

The binding of books has been described in detail because the finished products were so important to the children in my classroom.

Because this project was broken down into many small tasks, nearly every child was able to complete it easily. This fourth-grade classroom contained six children in the gifted and talented program, four children mainstreamed from learning-disabled, educable mentally retarded, and emotionally disturbed rooms, four children in speech and language therapy, and one bilingual child. All the children made Wisconsin "ABC" books of which they were very proud. Every child except one had all 26 pages in his or her book.

Cooperation in the classroom was excellent. Nearly every child served as an editor for peers; many children brought fabric to share; some helped cut wallpaper books. Others were great needle threaders or helped friends who were less able to sew, glue, or cut. Some of the children in the gifted and talented program gladly accepted help with illustrations from a talented artist in the learning-disabled program. Several of the average children, who often received less attention than those at either end of the spectrum, were excellent sewers or book assemblers and thus were much sought after.

Some of the most inarticulate children had some very successful pages. John, a child in the reading lab who had a difficult time in language arts, wrote:

tobacco
big, green
growing, planting, hanging
a lot of work
money

A major cash crop for farmers in our area of Wisconsin is tobacco, and John had just received a $600 check for his share of the family's tobacco income. This brought the study of Wisconsin's economy to him on a very meaningful level.

Others learned a great deal, too. When these children wrote, they were making judgments rather than just memorizing facts. They were evaluating which material to include in their writing. They were analyzing and synthesizing before arriving at a final written product. They were bringing their own experiences to the written work. Learning became unique and individualized for each child.

Writing has great value in the social studies curriculum. This particular use of poetry writing is one way to capitalize on writing as a technique for learning in social studies.

12. WRITING A THREE-PARAGRAPH REPORT

By Bernice Crane, Dorothy Lamb, and Jackie Martin

The chances that intermediate-grade students will be arrested for plagiarizing the World Book Encyclopedia are slim indeed. However, the penalties in our classroom for copying written assignments or reports directly from any encyclopedia, or even paraphrasing a published article, are almost as severe. Admittedly, writing such reports could be helpful as an exercise in penmanship if care is taken, and some learning might take place as a class listens to the report presented orally. However, if pupils merely copy their reports word for word from existing sources, their notion that encyclopedia writing is clear, concise, and accurate (good) while their own writing is confused, disorganized, and inaccurate (bad) is reinforced. Furthermore, they are encouraged to claim work done by others as their own, and their time is wasted. These negative results often accompany report writing in elementary school social studies because such writing all too often is actually nothing more than report copying.

Yet report writing is usually an important part of intermediate-grade social studies. We use an approach, called the three-paragraph report, which eliminates the possibility of copying and turns report writing into an activity of interest to our students. Using this procedure, students can learn to write using their own words and thoughts and putting information together in their own ways. By doing this, our students not only learn considerable social studies content but perfect their writing skills as well.

Writing a social studies report can serve a more valuable purpose than simply sharing facts with classmates; it can be a useful tool for helping young students organize their thinking. Instead of an exercise in rote learning, copying, and reciting, report writing can be a truly creative activity. The sense of pride students enjoy when they produce an original report is well worth the trouble it takes to help them write it. The problems they encounter in choosing a subject, selecting sources, taking notes, making an outline, writing a rough draft, editing, proofreading, and rewriting help them become better thinkers as well as better readers and writers.

The three-paragraph report is exactly what its name indicates--a report divided into three parts. Each part details one aspect of the main topic. Such a report can be prepared in a number of ways; as we have devised it, it consists of nine steps divided into three stages: prewriting, composing, and rewriting.

The prewriting stage actually consists of two different types of tasks. The first three steps essentially involve finding information to write about. The next two steps require students to process that information in order to produce significant ideas. The composing stage follows next, and the entire process concludes with the third stage--revising what has been written. We use the following guidelines as we help our fifth-graders move through these stages of the writing process:

Step 1: Choosing a Subject. Although the teacher may be tempted to assign specific subjects for students to write about, we believe that it is important for students to select their own topics. Part of the learning process is discovering whether a topic is too broad or too limited and whether relevant information is readily accessible.

A student's choice of subject should be based on his or her own interests or on those of the class as a whole. Certainly a report written by a student who is not interested in his or her topic will not be received with interest by the class. Thus, we allow as much latitude as possible on the choice of subject. A subject that is of great interest to the class but only slightly related to the unit of study is a better choice than a subject of little interest but absolute relevance. However, we allow no more than two or three reports on the same subject, so that the class will not become bored when the reports are shared.

Step 2: Identifying Sources. Since combining information from several sources is an important skill in writing reports, we require that each student use a minimum of three sources. To avoid relying on encyclopedias exclusively, we allow students to include only one encyclopedia among their sources. Obviously, we use our knowledge of the students' reading abilities to guide them to materials they can easily understand.

Students should be encouraged to use primary sources whenever possible, especially for writing in social studies. Live television coverage of news events can be an excellent source of up-to-date information. Interviews, too, provide interesting information about recent history. A report about World War II is livelier when it is based on a writer's conversation with a participant than when it is based on books alone. Surveys conducted by students to obtain information on various subjects--for example, job satisfaction, television viewing habits, and consumer preferences--are also useful. In addition, public records kept at the city hall or courthouse can be used to research such topics as community births and deaths, population growth, and property title transfers. Church records and cemetery lot records also contain an abundance of information that can be used in preparing reports on local history, as do local museums. Original documents, old newspapers, and letters are also useful sources that should not be overlooked.

Step 3: Taking Notes. We have our students take notes as they gather their information. They write their notes on three-by-five-inch cards because later in the process these notes will be sorted and shuffled according to subject. As a practical measure, sheets of notebook paper may be cut into small pieces and used in place of note cards. An envelope or rubber band is helpful in keeping notes together.

Students also use note cards to record summary sentences. If students have not had practice in writing sentences, some time is devoted to developing this skill. A chalkboard demonstration can be used for this purpose, with the teacher reading brief passages and asking the students to supply the key words that will invoke the same idea later. Once this skill has been sufficiently reviewed, the class is ready to take notes from the sources they have chosen for their reports.

To discourage students from copying a report word for word or simply paraphrasing, we do not permit them to write complete sentences on their note cards. The temptation to copy is great, so at this step we circulate among the students, marking out unnecessary words and phrases and emphasizing that only key words or phrases should be used. "Eggs about the size of small marbles" thus becomes "eggs size of marbles."

It is very important that each card contain only one idea. A minimum of 20 cards and a maximum of 40 will usually provide enough information for a good report. Students may find slightly different information on the same subject in different sources. They should be instructed to take notes from all sources, since they will be asked to integrate all this information as they organize their notes. In addition, they should make a separate note card containing the author's name, title, publisher, and date of publication for each source they use so that they can compile a simple bibliography for the reports.

Once students have collected the necessary information about their general topic, it is time to develop specific ideas. This aspect of prewriting requires students to play with the information as they search for interrelationships and big ideas.

Step 4: Organizing Notes. This step involves physically sorting the note cards into clusters of related data. For example, notes on Abraham Lincoln might be placed in separate groups related to his birth, family, education, early career, presidency, and death. This process helps students identify appropriate subtopics. A teacher should give as much assistance as necessary at this stage in order to help students decide which three subtopics will be most useful. The choice may be based on how much information exists in each category, on the extent of the students' interest in the various clusters, on how well the information in the three subtopics fits together, or on a combination of these considerations. It is likely that several cards will not be pertinent to any subtopic. Students should throw these away, no matter how painful the discarding process may be.

Any topic may be developed into a number of subtopics. Displaying some of the following examples on the chalkboard may be helpful to students as they choose their own subtopics.

Workers: administrators, producers, performers
City government: services, cost, control
Religion: need for, deities, forms of worship
Battle of Little Big Horn: reasons, personalities, outcome
Agriculture: history, tools, products
Vineyards: propagation, pruning, marketing

After the three subtopics have been selected, each student should organize the note cards within each subtopic. Students usually do not encounter much difficulty with this stage of preparation because by now they have become much more familiar with their subjects.

Step 5: Preparing the Outline. An outline is written from the note cards. Each of the three subtopics serves as a main idea in the outline. The cards within each subtopic can provide details in the outline to support the relevant main idea. Only rarely will it be necessary to divide these details into more specific details. For example, using the subtopics described in the Lincoln report, a student might choose education, presidency, and death as topics for his three paragraphs. An outline that might be developed from these ideas is shown below.

I. Education
  A. Less than year
  B. Borrowed books

II. Presidency
  A. 1861-1865
  B. Civil War
  C. Gettysburg Address

III. Death
  A. John Wilkes Booth
  B. Ford's Theater
  C. Funeral train
  D. Monument--Springfield, Illinois
  E. "O Captain, My Captain!"

The process of organizing note cards into three subtopic piles and then producing an outline based on these three piles of cards helps students organize their thoughts. This activity also helps students come up with ideas for topic sentences. After they have completed their outlines, they are ready to put pens to paper.

Step 6: Writing a First Draft. This step in writing a report involves developing paragraphs, using the main ideas and details from the outline. To rehearse this process, the class can work together to write a class report from a given outline after hearing a short article read aloud. Each section with a Roman numeral should become a fully developed paragraph, with a topic sentences based on the words or phrases following each Roman numeral and with details supplied from the outline and note cards. Students should be encouraged to add as much detail as possible from memory; thus, one note card may produce several sentences. On the other hand, if a student is able to supply only a few missing words to convert the information on the note card into a recognizable sentence, this effort should be enthusiastically welcomed as well.

The rough draft should be written on every other line, in order to provide space for revisions, additions, and corrections. To make the corrected copy easier to read, students should write on only one side of the paper. They should acknowledge the help they have received from their sources by including a simple bibliography.

A first draft, it should be noted, by no means constitutes a final product. Much remains to be done before a piece of writing can be considered "final." The remaining steps in the writing process consist of the feedback and revision needed to polish initial thoughts for final sharing with others.

Step 7: Getting Group Feedback. Feedback from peers is often helpful to a young writer in improving his or her writing. To provide for this kind of feedback, the class can be divided into small groups; each student can read his or her report aloud to a group. This step ensures that every report has an audience and permits the students to discover whether their intended audience will understand what they have to communicate. The group can also offer suggestions for improvement, especially if each critic is instructed to say three good things about the report before making a suggestion for improvement. Authors may or may not make revisions on the basis of these suggestions; the decision is theirs.

Step 8: Revising the Draft. The writer then rereads the draft, making whatever corrections or changes he or she feels are necessary. This scratched-out, written-over, working document can be examined for accuracy, clarity, and mechanics if the teacher wishes to do so. Such examination allows the teacher an opportunity to make suggestions without tracking red ink all over a paper that the student might consider a finished product, and it probably ensures that the final draft will be better than it would have been otherwise. By explaining the reasons for any corrections, the teacher can provide students with valuable help in developing the abilities to think and write clearly. Once the original drafts have been revised, students copy their reports neatly in ink on notebook paper. By this time, they have invested so much time, thought, and effort in their report that they should be motivated to work as carefully as they can.

Step 9: Sharing the Report. Perhaps the most fulfilling step in the sequence is sharing the finished reports with others. This can be done by reading them aloud to the class, displaying them on bulletin boards, binding them for a permanent classroom library, reading them over the school intercom, submitting them to children's publications, and sharing them at home. The sharing process allows students to show off their accomplishments and to receive assurances that all their work has been worthwhile. A paper tucked away in a folder, even with an "A" written in the corner, does not give the same feeling of satisfaction.

The teacher should judge each piece of writing according to the individual student's ability level. Abler students see the possibilities of such a report very quickly and tend to make more-sophisticated choices of subjects. Less-able students have more difficulty writing note cards, so only the simplest facts should be expected in their notes and reports. Since the requirement is three paragraphs instead of three pages, a teacher can accept very short, simple paragraphs from slow students and demand more-detailed paragraphs from the abler pupils. Thus, in a heterogenous class even the slow student has a chance to achieve success, while the gifted student is challenged.

Writing reports using the procedure described here can be as time consuming as a teacher wishes to make it. If time is limited, the following schedule might be used:

Day 1--Choose subject; visit library to check out books

Day 2--Take notes in class

Day 3--Take notes from noncirculating references in library

Day 4--Edit; proofread (teacher corrects, if time permits)

Day 5--Rewrite; share

An expanded timetable might look like this:

Day 1--Discuss topics; choose subject

Day 2--Give lesson on primary sources

Day 3--Review library techniques

Day 4--Demonstrate and practice note-taking skills

Day 5--Demonstrate and practice interviewing skills

Day 6--Take notes

Day 7--Take notes

Day 8--Take notes

Day 9--Demonstrate organization of note cards

Day 10--Give lesson on choosing subtopics

Day 11--Organize notes; choose subtopics; write outline

Day 12--Write rough draft

Day 13--Edit; proofread (teacher corrects, if time permits)

Whatever time is allotted, however, will be time well spent. Once students have learned to write three-paragraph reports using this method, they can easily use the same procedure for writing more-sophisticated reports in other subjects or at other grade levels.

13. LETTER WRITING IN THE INNER-CITY CLASSROOM

By Ellen Lazare Shatz

Slam! Bang! Crash! The classroom door opened with a clatter and two youngsters exploded into the room. "It came! It came! Mrs. Shatz, it really came. He wrote to us!"

The two boys ran around the room, their joy unbridled by the fact that they were in school. The rest of the class caught the spirit and began cheering. What could cause such excitement in a fifth-grade class? What could make generally unmotivated youngsters, who were basically turned off from learning, cheer in the middle of a dull, routine fifth-grade morning?

Philip and Gabriel had received a letter addressed to them from Herman Badillo, the first Puerto Rican to serve in the Congress of the United States. Several weeks before, the class had written letters to a number of prominent people asking how they had achieved the positions that they held. Here and now, at P.S. 89, two class members held in their hands a letter from a congressman answering their questions.

Philip and Gabriel read below grade level. They also experience difficulty in handling the day-to-day demands of being members of a class. Both boys are more capable than their records of academic achievement indicate, but they are embarrassed by the difficulty they have in reading. Class assignments and homework are seldom done. Whenever there is a problem--in the classroom, on the staircase, in the lunchroom, in the schoolyard--Philip and/or Gabriel can usually be relied on to be part of the problem. They don't like school. They seem ashamed if they become intrigued by an activity and actually get involved.

However, our letter-writing project seemed to capture their imaginations and overcome their fears. Herman Badillo was a man removed from school. Writing to him was an important adult, not childish, thing to do. The thought of writing to Herman Badillo, a prominent man in New York City and a hero to the Puerto Rican community, so captivated these youngsters that they worked diligently to write, revise, rewrite, and edit a thoughtful, questioning letter. How could a poor Puerto Rican boy in New York City become a congressman, a position of great prominence? How, in an establishment whose customs and language were so different from his own, did he "make it"? How could what Herman Badillo did influence the lives of two Puerto Rican boys from the Bronx?

Congressman Badillo sent a careful, caring response to the boys. He told them the story of his life. He talked about the difficulties of being poor and having dreams. He told them about really wanting to do something and working to that end, no matter how difficult it might seem. He sent them his picture and a Puerto Rican flag and told them to always be proud of their heritage.

This was not an instant success story. I am not able to report that Philip and Gabriel became model students and successful adults as a result of this experience. However, watching the youngsters and understanding some of what they learned from writing that letter--and receiving an answer--convinced me that this experience was a very important part of their education. Certainly it was the most educational experience that they had had in the fifth grade up to that point. They had sharpened their writing skills because they had something important to write. They used thinking skills to develop questions. They used research techniques to find out about Congressman Badillo. They read newspapers to learn about the local and national political scenes. They even actually wrote. But, most important of all, they developed power, because they had made a connection to Congressman Badillo. All because of doing some writing as a part of a social studies course.

When I planned the letter-writing project with that fifth-grade class, I was trying to inspire youngsters to write a well-planned, thoughtful letter. It probably was a good writing assignment, but it also taught me a lot about the power of letter writing.

We, as teachers and college graduates, probably were exposed to the power of the U.S. postal system well before we were aware of writing. As far back as I can remember, greeting cards were mailed and received for all occasions--birthdays, Christmas, Chanukah, Valentine's Day, graduations, engagements, weddings, and births. Letters were written to aunts, cousins, friends.

We write newsy letters, letters to record an event, and letters of inquiry. If we are angry or have a strong opinion, we know that we can express our feelings in a letter. We know that if we have something to say to a mayor, a congressman, or even to the president, we have a voice and a way of reaching that person. For us, letter writing is very much a part of our lives. We know that letter writing gives us power, a connection to anyone, even if we don't ever use it.

But not all people feel this way. People in the inner city, people from poor families, do not always share this power. Mail is not always a commonplace part of their lives. Inner-city children seldom receive mail addressed to them. Most of them don't have friends who live far away. They find it difficult to think of anything to say to someone they don't see. Most are not encouraged to write letters at home because stamps are expensive and letter writing is not an important part of their lives.

Although these children watch a great deal of television, they seldom watch the news. They often know the names of some public figures, but they seldom know what these people do or how prominent people can be connected to their own lives. The inner-city poor often feel that things "just happen" in this world. They feel that they have no power to change these happenings and that they have no voice.

Letter writing in school can give a child a voice. It can teach children that they have power as citizens and they can make connections to anyone. Letter writing is a powerful tool for connecting youngsters to the outside world.

This does not mean that youngsters can simply take pencil in hand and yell on paper. Letters are really an exercise in thinking. Letter writing is talking on paper. Letter writing involves becoming aware of what's happening that is personally meaningful. Letter writing requires thinking about why something evokes feelings and emotions as well as offering an opportunity to express feelings. Letter writing often involves trying to persuade someone else to change his or her mind. Letter writing also means that sometimes you will get a response and sometimes you will not.

It is good for children to know that people, even important people, do not always respond to letters. A letter writer must learn to evaluate the reasons why a letter wasn't answered. Was the message unclear? Was the tone of the letter too negative? Did the letter arrive at its destination? Once children learn to consider these questions, they will want to review and revise their letters to make them clear, helpful, and easy to read. They will learn the importance of proper form, good handwriting, and carefully addressed envelopes.

Writing letters gives children a clear sense of audience. They know exactly who will read the letters, and they can address their remarks directly to those persons. The writer's knowledge of the intended recipient affects what is said in a letter and how it is said.

One year my third-grade class was particularly fascinated with the writings of Dr. Seuss. They loved hearing and reading his eloquent silliness. His word games skipped off their tongues as they experimented with reading his writing aloud. I suggested to the children that they do something special to celebrate the birthday of Dr. Seuss. Being very much in tune with Dr. Seuss, the youngsters decided to write to him.

The children wrote letters and birthday cards to send to their favorite author. In their writings they used made-up words and rhythmic sound patterns, just as Dr. Seuss does in his writing. The youngsters had a very strong sense of Dr. Seuss as an audience, and they were able to direct their writing to him.

Writing letters forces students to think about a specific audience. It teaches them to use their inner voices to direct their messages to the persons who are going to read their letters. As they continue writing letters, they become more aware that letter writing is inner speech written on paper and that eventually this principle can be applied to other kinds of writing. They must think: What do I want to say to this person--what do I really want to say?

When a letter is mailed, it is carrying a part of the writer. Therefore, it becomes important to the writer to get it just right. The writer has to look at the letter and think, "Who would write this? How does it sound? Is that the way I want it to sound?" Often a student will revise and rewrite until the letter sounds just right.

Then the child can address himself or herself to the way the letter looks. Youngsters can understand the need of proper form in friendly letters as well as business letters. They can understand the necessity of including a clear inside address, if they want a response. Their letters are part of them--their voices reaching out to others. Just as a visitor tries to make a good impression, young letter writers often feel impelled to edit, to make sure that spelling and punctuation are correct. Good clear handwriting becomes important. Children learn that when you mail a letter, sending away a piece of your writing, you are sending away a piece of yourself.

Letter writing gives children a voice. It makes them feel powerful. They can say something by letter to someone whom they might not otherwise touch. Letters are tools that are helpful in giving youngsters an opportunity to write about their feelings. Letters give youngsters connections to the outside world. Letters help children become personally tied in to the 6 o'clock news and to their government and to the happenings in their world.

As a classroom teacher, I try to capitalize on all events that can help the youngsters reach out into the world. When U.S. citizens were captured and held as hostages in Iran, one class wrote letters to cheer them up. When the hostages were released the following year, my class watched this event on television. The youngsters were very moved by what they saw. They talked about their feelings and wrote letters.

> Dear Friend,
> I am so glad you're back. I am wearing a yellow ribbon. At last, there is freedom, at last there is happiness. I don't know why the Iranians captured you, but I am so glad you're back. I will say it differently. The way Dr. Martin Luther King, Jr. said it "Free at last, free at last. Thank God Almighty we are free at last."
> Love,
> Nana-kofi

> Dear Friend,
> How are you feeling? I hope you feel good. I am happy that you all have freedom. It is good to be free and I am happy for all of you. I hope that you are happy too. I hope you have a good home and a good life.
> Your friend,
> Kim

The results of letter writing can be surprising. During the last week of school, Robert received the following answer to his letter, which he shared with his classmates:

DEPARTMENT OF STATE
Washington, D.C. 20520

Dear Robert,

I want to tell you how much I appreciated your words of welcome home and to thank you for your support and your prayers during all the long months of captivity in Iran.

Nothing has been so reassuring to me than to see how the young people of our country have found reason in this experience to renew their commitment to the principles of freedom and liberty and human decency on which our country's future rests.

You make me proud to be an American and you make me confident that our country's future is bright. I hope you will keep an open heart and mind toward Iran so that in time our two countries can again be friends.

God bless you and keep you.

Sincerely,
L. Bruce Laingen

P.S. Sorry to be so long in replying to your nice letter. I really enjoyed reading it and hope you will also give my best regards to Mrs. Shatz and to all of your classmates.

In March 1981, President Ronald Reagan was wounded in an assassination attempt. The youngsters in class 4-40 watched television, talked, and wrote some letters:

Dear President Reagan:

I was very sad when I heard that you were shot, but I hope that you are feeling better when you get this letter. I hope it was nothing serious. I hope Mr. Brady gets better too.

I don't think people should hurt or kill anyone because the world was made to share and enjoy with others.

I'm hoping you get better.

Yours truly,
David

Dear President Reagan:

I hope that you are better now. I hope that you will be out of the hospital soon. I wonder why you were shot. It is dangerous to carry guns. Why do people shoot people? I hope you get better soon.

Love,
Joy

On April 28, 1981, a second-grader from Rockville Center, Long Island, became a nationwide celebrity. During his first public appearance after the shooting, at a joint session of the Congress, President

Reagan thanked the American people for all their good wishes and read a letter from young Peter Sweeney.

The youngsters in my class had received a thank-you note from the president. However, on the morning after Peter Sweeney's letter was read on national television, the members of class 4-40 were elated. They, too, had made an important connection to the White House and to the president of the United States. Nothing better demonstrates the value of letter writing in elementary school social studies.

14. USING WRITING TO CONDUCT A FANTASY FIELD TRIP

By Carol Palay

Field trips involve the senses in ways that no textbook can. After venturing beyond the school grounds, students often return to their classrooms more motivated to discover what they can learn from their books and teachers. Recognizing this truism, I one day eagerly planned to take my 11th-grade American Civilization students on a field trip to Williamsburg, Virginia. Since our school is located within a four-hour drive of Williamsburg, we thought we would get an early start, spend the day, and return that evening. However, we were sorely disappointed when the school administration denied our field-trip request because of lack of funds. We groaned and complained, expecting that our study of colonial life in America would have to be relegated to a few dull chapters in the text.

Fortunately, this did not happen. I discovered that one of my colleagues possessed 50 slides of Williamsburg, purchased on a previous visit there. However, rather than simply show the slides to the class while lecturing about facts of interest, I decided to use them as "artifacts" and let the students dig up relevant information which they, in turn, would present to the class. We would be able to "visit" Williamsburg even though we could not leave the school.

Thus was born our "fantasy field trip." Although my experience involved secondary students, with some modification elementary school teachers can readily adapt this technique to their specific age groups and subjects.

First, I allowed my students to divide themselves into groups of five or six. Each group chose a leader and selected a place in Williamsburg that particularly interested them, such as the Raleigh Tavern, the Governor's Palace, or the Apothecary Shop. I then gave each group appropriate slides--usually three or four for each site--and the following instructions:

> Study these slides by observing them and listing details that will vividly describe them. Infer the purpose and/ or function of the places you observe. You will additionally research a related topic of colonial life around 1750 which is relevant to your location. (For example, the courthouse group will be responsible for researching colonial crimes and punishment.)
>
> Your objective is to write a script that includes this information. You will later tape the script which, in its final form, will provide a guided, informative tour through the slides of your Williamsburg site.

Essentially, each group was to create its own learning station. The culminating event would be a visit to all stations and, consequently, a tour of the major sites in Williamsburg.

The knowledge that their audience would consist of their own classmates fired a friendly competition between groups which resulted in many creative touches far beyond my own expectations. At the beginning of each class period, I assigned specific objectives for that day. Group leaders were responsible for guiding their groups in accomplishing all the tasks necessary for the finished project as well as for keeping me informed of their groups' progress.

After explaining to the class what the final outcome of the project should be, I gave each group a list of tasks. The group leaders helped their members split up these assignments and then submitted lists of their members' duties. Because some of the jobs involved more time and effort than others, people doubled up on some tasks. Conversely, it was sometimes possible for one person to handle several jobs. What was important, however, was that the students, not the teacher, decided how each group would operate, with the understanding that the final grade depended on sharing as well as accepting responsibility.

In addition to preparing descriptions of each slide and doing the related research, each group had to produce a sign for its location, a colonial culinary confection selected from a collection of authentic 18th- century recipes, and a poster displaying the recipe and its source. However, writing the script for the slides was the central task of each group. This involved organizing the research, creating the script, and, finally, producing a clear tape recording. I encouraged each group to listen as one member read the draft script aloud. In this way, errors in grammar, logic, sequence, and content could be noted and corrected.

Moreover, I asked that all the scripts be uniform in length--four to six minutes. This time restriction forced the students to reread and revise their scripts in order to meet the requirement. As I circulated in the classroom during this phase of the activity, I heard group members commenting, "Slow down--you're reading too fast" or "We need more material; this just isn't going to last four minutes." This was a natural solution to the problem of teaching students to take a second or even a third look at what they have written. Besides, students themselves tend to be the toughest critics. Aware of keen peer scrutiny, the groups worked very hard on the revisions so that their final scripts would run smoothly and hold an attentive audience.

The students showed off their abilities to entertain an audience by presenting their information in many imaginative ways. The Governor's Mansion group provided harpsichord music as a background for its script. When visiting the Raleigh Tavern, tourists heard a rousing 18th-century drinking tune sung by enthusiastic students. At the College of William and Mary, the tour guide interviewed historical graduates who told us of challenging curriculum and difficult examinations. Even the sign making became an exciting opportunity. We knew we had come to the Williamsburg "gaol" when our eyes met a wooden post inscribed by a student in her wood-burning class. The sign at the George Wythe house was a blueprint of the home drawn by a student aspiring to become an architect. He also brought information on Georgian architecture to his group which was integrated into the script.

In addition to the 11 groups working on various Williamsburg locations, a 12th group was assigned the role of Chamber of Commerce. This group worked to unify the project and to provide background information for the tourists. The Chamber of Commerce learning station was different in that it was solely visual. Using charts, diagrams and drawings, its creators illustrated the city history (how and when it was founded), its population around 1750, its leading citizens, its contacts with England and other colonies, its ethnic groups, its major industry and crops, its religious makeup, and the role of slavery in the community. A highlight of this group's work was a wall-size map of Williamsburg showing the points of interest on our class tour. The Chamber of Commerce publicized our tour by extending invitations to faculty, administrators, and other students outside of our own class. The group tackled this assignment by first researching colonial calligraphy, then writing invitations which they duplicated, folded, and stamped with sealing wax, all according to proper colonial etiquette.

My students became totally involved in the field-trip production, thereby creating a learning experience marked by their own individual talents. I worked with my students, welcoming their suggestions along the way, so that the tour would belong to all of us.

Just as my students' ideas made our field trip unique, so would a different class be able to design its own version. Although I taught in an open-space school and had a large area that could accommodate 12 learning stations, a regular classroom could contain five or six stations, which would still allow for a diverse tour. Other classes could contribute different stations, if they wished, and all students could benefit from the work of students outside of their own class.

Finding time to prepare the trip is not necessarily a problem. My special circumstances included a two-hour block which enabled me to consolidate a schedule. However, since much of the research and preparation of materials was done outside of class, the entire activity could be completed in approximately seven regular (50-minute) high school class periods. (Upper-elementary-school students might require somewhat more time.) I followed this schedule for in-class work:

1 hour:	selection of groups, assignment of tasks, preview of slides
1½ hours:	research in school library
1½ hours:	group coordination of research into polished scripts, including practice readings and revisions
½ hour:	setting up of stations, signs and wall decorations
2 hours:	field-trip experience; all students circulated through all 12 stations
¼ hour:	self-evaluation

Finally, we required certain materials. For each group I needed a slide projector and a tape recorder. My students supplied their own blank tapes, which I returned after the field trip. In addition, we used extension cords, construction paper, masking tape, and white paper for screens. When we finally collected everything we needed, the results were impressive indeed.

On the day of our "fantasy field trip," the classroom bustled with last-minute preparations. Leaders checked to be sure their stations had all the necessary items: slides, recorder, tape, and script (in case of technical difficulties with audiovisual equipment). Then we were ready. With the lights out, we began our journey. After five or six minutes, a flashing of the lights signaled that it was time to move on to the next location.

As a result of this experience, the students agreed, they had learned a great deal about Williamsburg. Some were even eager to organize their own family excursions there. However, I believe that the value of this project was not so much in its outcome as in its evolution. My students sharpened their research, organization, composition, and revision skills. They learned how to cooperate in a group and how to accept responsibility; if someone was not producing what he or she had promised, group pressure clearly communicated that this was unacceptable behavior. More often, groups supported their members for their contributions, thus bolstering each student's knowledge of his or her own self-worth.

I am convinced that the reason why the students felt comfortable in the group setting was because of the diversity of tasks, each requiring different kinds of skills. This allowed students to select tasks best suited to their strengths. For example, one boy, generally not academically motivated, displayed his technical prowess by managing all the AV equipment for his group. Another student diligently practiced reading his group script aloud until he felt satisfied that he could produce a professional-sounding tape recording. Others, more artistically inclined, designed signs and recipe posters, while would-be chefs combed our library's historic cookbook section for exciting recipes. Inquisitive students immediately headed for the library to research information they needed for their scripts. For the most part, my students realized that some jobs required more work than others, and that the amount of time and effort spent would readily show up in the final product. Hence, grades were relative, with students, in effect, deciding their own grades on the basis of how they had chosen to contribute to their groups.

I was pleased to watch <u>all</u> my students actively participating. How proud they were when visiting administrators and faculty members sat down at their stations! They were even more delighted when another social studies teacher borrowed their tapes and scripts so that she could set up the field trip for use in her own classroom.

I was even more pleased by the opportunities this project provided for students to use and improve their writing skills. When asked to write a composition, students often lose sight of the process every writer must encounter; they became anxious about producing the <u>final</u> paper. But writing was such an integral part of this project that students actually became willing participants in writing without even realizing it. While looking at the slides, group members noted and then pooled the visible details about a room. Next, assuming the role of docent, they arranged those details into narratives so that their scripts would guide the eyes of other students around the room. Furthermore, in the process of researching topics related specifically to their slides, students gathered information which they wove into their narratives. For example, one room in the Brush Everard house had a fine display of children's toys. My students could clearly describe the playroom, but they felt that their description was inadequate without further explanation of how the toys were used. After some research, they expanded their notes on colonial childhood pastimes into colorful sentences and added them to the narrative.

The first drafts of the scripts revealed several common traits: they were written in several hands, in ink and in pencil; they were full of scratchouts, from single words to entire paragraphs; they were marred by misspellings and grammatical errors, and they lacked transitional continuity. However, after many practice readings of the scripts, most errors were corrected and transitions from slide to slide were supplied. Students who rarely took the time to go over their written work were recognizing the benefits of reading and listening to it. They discovered that they could <u>hear</u> mistakes better than they could see them. There was also a desire within each group to create the very best script possible. Being thus motivated to excel, the students became effective editors of each other's work. They searched for the "right" word by asking their fellow group members for suggestions. Dictionaries and grammar books were consulted with little prodding from me. One student in each group recopied the script, which was once again criticized and tightened up by the group the next day. When a script was finally accepted by the group as the final draft, it was taped. In this manner my students had practiced all the necessary skills which lead to polished writing.

The destination for a fantasy field trip can be anyplace--perhaps an Indian reservation or even the solar system! A trip can be easily modified to suit the age of the students and the subject they are studying. Slides may be replaced by pictures, photographs, or real objects, or the students themselves can draw or construct the "artifacts" that will provide the basis for a script at each station. The process I have described is highly adaptable because any school-age child can benefit from group interaction and prepare and tape a script.

Learning centers are not a new idea. What is new about this idea is that the teacher allows the students to create them, thereby involving class members in an activity that calls upon their own resourcefulness. Our fantasy field trip engaged students in all the major steps of the writing process. They actually enjoyed writing to learn social studies content--and they improved their writing in the process.

15. WRITING TO LEARN ABOUT DEMOCRACY

By Betty Dyarmett

A sea of puzzled fifth-grade faces filled the classroom one Monday morning. Why the puzzlement? Posters displayed around the room announced "Trial of Socrates Coming Soon" and asked "Is Socrates Innocent or Guilty?" Thus began a series of lessons involving writing which were developed for our fifth-grade basic social studies curriculum unit on ancient Greece. The initial idea had grown out of my work the previous year in cooperation with a student teacher, Hope Strainer.

Our overall content goal was to compare and contrast ancient and contemporary democracies. To make this subject more relevant to 9- and 10-year-olds, we decided to have the students prepare and conduct two mock trials of Socrates--one to be set in ancient Athens and the other in the contemporary United States. Central to this unit were to be student-prepared scripts. Our students would use writing as a basis for thinking and speaking about justice in ancient Greece and the United States today.

Our writing could not begin until we had collected considerable background information. Hope and I made charts displaying introductory information related to the three branches of government in ancient Athens and in modern America--executive, legislative, and judicial. This information provided a starting point for an in-depth study of the two judicial systems.

We spent three days hearing oral reports by several students on the workings of the U.S. justice system. Resource people from the community also came to give first-hand information concerning the courts. Whitney's father, an attorney, answered many questions about court proceedings. These people provided the students with a basic understanding of how our courts operate and a familiarity with some basic legal terminology.

Next it was time to delve into reference books, with the assistance of the school librarian, to find out about ancient Greece. (A list of useful resources for student researchers is included at the end of this chapter.) The children gathered information which would be transformed into their own informal scripts for mock trials of Socrates under the Athenian and American systems.

In order to help students focus on the task, we assigned each one a specific role, partly on the basis of reading ability. (Because of the limited material on Socrates written at a fifth-grade level, the more difficult individual roles were given to the better readers.) All students received roles which required summarizing some reference material, and every member of the class had at least one role. Some were specific individuals. Others sat on the juries. Some students portrayed individual characters as well as participating as jurors.

We developed a set of role cards to guide the students in writing their individual parts (see Figure 4). The questions on the role cards were designed to help the students understand their roles in the trials and develop their characters' points of view.

The students spent two days searching for information and taking notes. After they had answered the questions on their role cards, the children met in groups to coordinate, write, and edit their scripts. The class was divided into the following four groups:

Group 1 (American): defense witness and attorney, judge, three jurors.

Group 2 (American): witnesses and attorney for the prosecution, Socrates, three jurors.

Group 3 (Athenian): Socrates, witness for Socrates, four jurors.

Group 4: Bailiff, witness against Socrates, four jurors (two American and two Athenian).

The students did not actually write complete scripts for the trials; each one prepared a script for his or her role. I explained that the students could refer to or even read from their scripts during the trials; they did not have to memorize their parts. I also explained that they did not have to copy other students' parts. I did ask the attorneys and witnesses to coordinate and sequence their questions and answers and to let the judge know what they had decided. Our background study and research had made the students sufficiently familiar with the trial formats so that they had no problems knowing how the various parts would fit together. For example, in the Athenian trial the only speeches required were by Socrates and those speaking for and against him. In the American trial, however, more characters were involved, so a sequence sheet was developed which indicated the order in which people would be participating.

After drafts of the individual scripts had been completed, the students shared them with their groups for feedback concerning meaning, accuracy, and clarity. Then they rewrote their scripts, making revisions on the basis of this feedback. On the following day, the groups met again to check their final scripts for capitalization, punctuation, and spelling; I provided assistance when needed. Corrections were then made on the final draft. After these final sessions, we rehearsed each trial. We were then ready to try out the trials on an audience.

Visiting classes were greeted at the door and led to seats in the crowded classroom. Teachers were given signs to wear identifying them as representatives of "NBC News," "ABC News," and "CBS News" during the American trial.

The Athenian trial began with a witness speaking in favor of Socrates. Next, a witness speaking against Socrates accused him of corrupting youth and being unfaithful to the gods. As Socrates, Christopher then spoke in his own defense, using quotes from the original speech. The scripts written earlier proved most useful to all involved.

Because an Athenian jury consisted of between 201 and 1,001 jurors, everyone in the room, including the visitors, became Athenian jurors. By a show of hands, a majority of the jury found Socrates guilty and sentenced him to death by drinking hemlock. Socrates was given a cup of water, and after staggering around the room for several seconds, he dropped to the floor. The students really got into the spirit of the activity!

Discussion followed. The class examined Socrates's decision to die for what he believed rather than live out his life in exile. We discussed what values the students would be willing to die for; the answers included "my mother," "my brother," "my family," "my dog," "my country," and "freedom."

Figure 4

ROLE CARDS FOR MOCK TRIALS OF SOCRATES

Socrates
(Athenian trial)

1. Why are you on trial?
2. How do you feel about what people think of you?
3. Use Socrates' speech from the textbook to plan your defense.

Socrates
(American trial)

1. Why are you on trial?
2. What are some of the things you have been doing and saying?

Judge
(American trial)

1. What does <u>overrule</u> mean?
2. What does <u>sustained</u> mean?
3. What will you do and say if the courtroom gets noisy?
4. What will your sentence be if Socrates is found guilty?
5. What will you say if Socrates is innocent?

Attorney for the Defense
(American trial)

1. What does <u>attorney for the defense</u> mean?

2. What is the First Amendment?

3. What are some questions you can ask to prove that Socrates is innocent?

4. What is your closing statement? Use the First Amendment to help you.

5. When you are finished, meet with the defense witnesses in the American trial.

Attorney for the Prosecution
(American trial)

1. What does <u>attorney for the prosecution</u> mean?

2. What is Socrates guilty of?

3. What are some questions you can ask to show that Socrates is guilty?

4. What is your closing statement?

5. Meet with the prosecution witnesses in the American trial when you are finished.

Witness for the Defense
(American and Athenian trials; separate card for each)

1. What does <u>witness for the defense</u> mean?

2. How do you feel about what Socrates is doing?

3. What are some of the things he has said and done for you to be on his side?

Witness for the Prosecution
(American and Athenian trials; separate card for each)

1. What does witness for the prosecution mean?
2. How do you feel about what Socrates is doing?
3. What are some of the things you have seen Socrates do?
4. What are some of the things you have heard Socrates say?

Jury
(Athenian trial)

1. What is Socrates accused of doing?
2. As an Athenian freeman, how do you feel about what Socrates has done?
3. How will you vote? Innocent or guilty?
4. How will you show your vote?

Jury
(American trial)

1. What are your responsibilities in this case?
2. What does innocent mean?
3. What does guilty mean?
4. How will you show your vote?

Spokesman for the Jury
(American trial)

1. What is your job?

2. What does innocent mean?

3. What does guilty mean?

4. What will you say when the judge asks for your verdict? Remember that there are two choices.

Bailiff
(American trial)

1. What is a bailiff?

2. What are your duties during the trial?

3. What do you say when a witness comes to the stand?

4. What prop do you need?

The American trial began with the bailiff asking everyone to stand as the judge entered the room. Kevin looked very authentic in his long black robe. Subsequently, witnesses were sworn in by the bailiff, examined, and cross-examined. Judge Cox at times had to overrule an attorney's objection, as when the prosecuting attorney asked a witness for the defense, "Have you ever gone around town talking out of your head like Socrates?"

Carl had written Socrates's original speech in today's language. It included such statements as: "I was just standin' on the corner talkin' to a bunch of kids. That's not against the law. I have the right to freedom of speech, don't I?" The case was argued from the standpoint of upholding the First Amendment.

After closing arguments by both attorneys, the jury was asked to leave the room to reach its verdict. This time only 12 jurors were involved. When they returned to the classroom after several minutes of deliberation, Judge Cox called Socrates to the bench and asked the jury, "How do you find the defendant, guilty or not guilty?"

"Not guilty, Your Honor," responded Ernest, spokesman for the jury.

Cheers, shouts, and applause filled the courtroom, with only a few scattered boos. Banging his gavel, the judge brought the court to order and declared, "Case dismissed!"

During the discussion that followed, students compared and contrasted the Athenian and American justice systems, identifying the advantages and disadvantages of each. The students concluded that in the Athenian democracy more people could act as jurors and represent the public, while in the United States the judge knows the laws and is fairer in passing sentences. They also decided that the size of a country is a factor in the operation of its government. Changes through the centuries in people's attitudes toward individual rights were also discussed.

The day after the American trial, epitaphs for Socrates were written on construction paper cut in the shape of tombstones. These were then placed on the bulletin board for all to enjoy. Two of the epitaphs were "He died for what he believed in" and "He only spoke the truth."

In the space of nine days, the class had researched and dramatized the trials of Socrates. More important, the students had learned about democracy.

Writing played a central role in this social studies learning experience. The process of writing the scripts not only motivated students' research, it served as a vehicle for coming to grips with the major subject of study and for forming and communicating ideas about the subject. Comparisons between ancient and contemporary democracies were made more meaningful to the students. The prewriting activities of researching and answering questions enabled students to focus on the specifics of the project.

Reading parts orally in peer groups allowed for constructive feedback to each individual student. Frequently, errors in punctuation, omission of words, and awkward construction were recognized by the readers themselves. The importance of clear and precise writing was made evident as peers reacted to each piece of writing.

Peer groups also provided aid in proofreading and revising individual drafts. Students were then more confident and eager to rewrite their final scripts. This process exemplifies the unit concept of individuals together making a democracy work.

The writing of epitaphs required students to summarize their conceptions of the life of Socrates. This activity proved valuable in solidifying the meaning of democracy.

Thus, student writing was the core of this unit. Certainly the activities we undertook had some rough edges--edges that can be polished as the unit is revised and repeated. However, even in their unfinished stages these mock trials demonstrate a strategy that permits students to write to learn content in elementary school social studies and to practice some of the very concepts they are learning about.

Resources for Students

Bostick, Nancy, et al. *Greek and Roman Civilization*. Boston: Allyn and Bacon, 1975. (The history and organization of Athenian democracy; the life and trial of Socrates.)

Brindze, Ruth. *All About Courts and the Land*. New York: Random House, 1964. (Organization of courts and glossary of legal terms.)

Coolidge, Olivia. *The Golden Days of Greece*. New York: Thomas Y. Crowell, 1968. (The life and trial of Socrates.)

Katz, William Loren, and Bernard Gaughran. *The Constitutional Amendments*. New York: Franklin Watts, 1974. (A description of the amendments.)

Morris, Richard B. The First Book of the Constitution. New York: Franklin Watts, 1958. (An introduction to the Constitution and contents of the amendments.)

Robinson, Charles Alexandria, Jr. The First Book of Ancient Greece. New York: Franklin Watts, 1960. (An easy-to-read book on ancient Greece and the life of Socrates.)

Uviller, H. Richard. "Courts." In The New Book of Knowledge, vol. 4. New York: Grolier, 1978. (Description of the proceedings of a court trial.)

Van Duyan, Janet. The Greeks: Their Legacy. New York: McGraw-Hill, no date. (Ancient Greek history and the life of Socrates.)

16. LEARNING TO WRITE IN "SMALL BITES"

By Janet Cuenca

In my 20 years as a teacher of language arts and social studies, I have spent much time trying to resolve the dilemma every teacher faces: how to get the best results from my students without working myself to death at home. I know what's good for my students: they should be encouraged to think and write about content material every day. They should get immediate feedback on their efforts, and they should be given time to revise what they have written and to correct errors in mechanics and content. But I know what's good for me, too: I should be able to spend my evenings and weekends living my own life. I need to read, spend time with my family, travel, and tend my garden, not spend every minute grading stacks of papers.

I have evolved a sequence of lesson-steps which has helped me to resolve this dilemma. If I am to use writing well, it seems to me that the solution is to break down a writing effort into a series of short, easily learned, and easily evaluated tasks. Students can write each day, but I don't have to carry the work home with me to evaluate it. It is a humane system for both students and teacher. The key to this system is underlining.

The set of tasks involved in underlining lessons should be carried out in sequence. However, it is not intended that the full sequence be carried out every time students write. Rather, the sequence can be used step by step as a device to teach students each stage in creating a good composition. The sequence, in whole or in part, can also be repeated as often as a teacher wishes, considering the time available or students' needs for reinforcement. Finally, this series of steps can easily be carried out while a class is engaged in activities related to any social studies unit.

Before beginning to use underlining lessons, it may be helpful to understand the answers to three major questions about them. First, with what problem is underlining designed to deal? Second, how are these lessons created and presented? And third, how can underlining lessons be used in the classroom?

Underlining lessons are designed to correct the tendency to include irrelevant material in an essay. I found that students included "everything but the kitchen sink" in their essays. If a piece of information was included in the reading which accompanied the question, students felt justified in using it, whether or not it pertained to the question. For example, on one occasion my students were assigned to explain why the ancient Romans had built their extensive network of roads. The reading explained this clearly, but it also included material on the steps involved in actually constructing roads. The vast majority of students devoted more space to telling how the Romans built roads than to the information required by the question.

I designed my first underlining lesson to correct this error in thinking. I gave each student two identical copies of the reading. On one copy I asked the students to underline sentences that told how the Romans built roads. On the other, they were asked to underline sentences that told why the Romans built roads. After discussion and correction of errors, students could lay the two readings side by side and have a visual reminder that more than one essay could be written from a single set of information. This process helped them to see that a text gives information about many aspects of a topic.

To further explain this concept, I used the analogy of a toy box. In a toy box one might find Tinker Toys, Lego bricks, Lincoln Logs, dolls, and little cars and trucks. These items all belong in the toy box because they are all toys. Similarly, both kinds of information belongs in the reading about ancient Roman roads because the reading is all about Roman roads. All the toys in the toy box are fun to play with, and all the facts about the Roman roads are interesting to know. However, suppose a teacher gives a young child the toy box with the instruction to build something with the Tinker Toys. If the child then includes some of the Lincoln Logs or Lego bricks in the project, the teacher has a problem: Did the child deliberately ignore the directions, or is it that he or she genuinely cannot tell the difference between Tinker Toys, Lincoln Logs, and Lego bricks? A student who includes the wrong information in an essay creates the same dilemma: Did the student ignore the question, or is it that he or she genuinely cannot distinguish between general information and that which specifically answers the assigned question? My students responded well to the toy-box analogy. Now, when I give my students an underlining assignment, I tell them, "Remember! Use only the Tinker Toys!"

Underlining lessons are not difficult to make and present. The basic steps are obvious: select a reading, type it, and duplicate it. However, the lessons might take various forms. One form is to give each student two identical copies of the same reading, and ask the students to underline material for two different questions. Another form is to give each student one copy of the reading and just one question. A third form is to present the lesson at different levels of difficulty in order to accommodate low-ability students. The majority of students get the full reading, while low-ability students receive a shorter version of the same selection.

Regardless of what form the underlining lesson takes, the following points should be kept in mind:

--The reading should always contain more information than is needed to answer the question, so that the students need to think about what to use and what to discard.

--The passage should focus on a major point of the unit, so that it reinforces content that you'd need to emphasize in any case.

--The patterns of the lessons should be varied; one time a great deal of information would be underlined, the next time very little. On one occasion the material to be underlined might be all together in the middle or at the end; on the next day the material to be underlined might be interspersed throughout the reading. If only one pattern is used, students tend to underline sentences according to the pattern they expect to see.

Underlining lessons may be used in a variety of ways in the classroom. An underlining exercise is an excellent way to begin a writing project. Papers can be evaluated very quickly by the teacher (at about the rate of two per minute, with an answer key) or they can be discussed as soon as everyone has finished underlining and evaluated later.

In any case, a follow-up discussion is crucial. Students should verbalize why a sentence is underlined--or not underlined. (Explaining why not is as important as explaining why.) For example, in a discussion about the Tasaday's stone tools, it is important that students see that they should not underline sentences about the device for making fire. (That tool is made of wood, not stone, and the question specifies stone tools.) Students who made that error will read questions more carefully in the future. On the sample handout in Figure 5, one sentence is enclosed in brackets. These brackets indicate a sentence which might or might not be underlined. A person could give good arguments for excluding it as well as for including it. In such a case, I count the answer neither right nor wrong, and I try to get a good discussion going in the class. As the sentences are discussed, each student should underline sentences which he or she overlooked and erase the lines from wrongly underlined sentences. (That's why it's important to do the work in pencil, rather than ink or crayon.) If students are going to go on to write essays in answer to a question, it's important that they end up with properly underlined readings to work from.

An underlining lesson is useful even if there will be no follow-up essay. The underlining process itself forces students to think about the material they are reading; it is an excellent exercise in reading comprehension, and it reinforces whatever social studies concepts are being emphasized in that part of the unit.

The sample lessons outlined below illustrate each step in the writing process I have been using successfully with fourth-graders. The content was taken from a fourth-grade social studies writing project on "The Tasaday's Stone Tools." Teachers of older or younger students can adapt these procedures to fit the needs of their students.

Step 1: Underlining Relevant Information. Give each student a copy of a short reading, taken from their text or from an appropriate supplementary resource. (The handout given to students at this point is reproduced in Figure 5. Only the answer key is reproduced here; the student copy is not underlined.) Go over the directions with the class, emphasizing that the underlining should be done in pencil. As the students complete this task, check their underlined sentences against your copy of the answer key. When all the students have finished, go over the reading with the entire class and ask for reasons why each sentence

Figure 5

STUDENT HANDOUT FOR UNDERLINING EXERCISE

Directions: You may soon be asked to write a short essay about the stone tools used by the Tasaday. This assignment will help you prepare to write. First, read the entire passage below. Then reread it to look for the sentences which give information on this topic. Finally, underline in pencil each sentence that contains information that you could use in writing about this topic.

Tasaday Tools Before Dafal*

[When Dafal met the Tasaday, they were using tools made of stone. Probably, these tools were like the tools their ancestors had used.] People thousands of years ago used stone tools. These people were called Stone Age people. Some social scientists think the Tasaday were living like the Stone Age people.

The Tasaday used a hammer ax to pound bark from tree trunks. This tool was made from a smooth stone shaped like an egg. It was tied to a short wooden handle.

Another Tasaday tool was a long, flat stone with one sharp edge. It, too, had a short wooden handle. The Tasaday used this tool to cut rattan (ra tan') into strips. Rattan is a climbing palm tree. It has long, tough stems. The Tasaday used the strips of rattan to tie the handles on the stone tools.

The Tasaday also had a small, flat stone with a sharp edge. This tool is called a scraper. Before they had bolos, the scraper was their most important tool. The Tasaday used the scraper to shape pieces of bamboo into digging sticks and knives.

To make the stone tool, the Tasaday would first find a stone that was the right size. They might grind one edge against another stone. This would make it sharp.

To make a fire, the Tasaday used two pieces of wood. They put a long round stick in a dent on a thicker stick. The men took turns rolling the round stick between their palms until smoke appeared. Then, they touched a piece of dry moss to the hot stick. They blew on the moss until it flamed.

---

*Reprinted from Studying Cultures (McGraw-Hill Social Studies), by J.L. Tucker, R. Messick, C. Cherryholmes, and G. Manson, copyright 1979, with the permission of Webster/McGraw-Hill.

should or should not have been underlined. During this process, students can correct their own papers---erasing the "wrong" underlines and adding those that they missed.

Step 2: Writing a Topic Sentence. Explain that the handouts from the underlining exercise will be useful in writing a short essay, and that the assignment will be "Describe two of the Tasaday's stone tools." Point out that this topic is almost the same as the one used in the underlining activity; in this case, however, the students will be writing about only two stone tools. Tell the students to begin by writing a topic sentence that will introduce an essay about any two stone tools used by the Tasaday. (This step is based on the assumption that the students have already learned how to recognize and compose a topic sentence.) Announce that every acceptable topic sentence will be graded "A"; others will not receive a grade. When the students have finished writing their topic sentences and gone on to other seat work, go from desk to desk and grade their sentences.

In grading the topic sentences and the "detail" sentences that students will write later, it is important to be lenient about minor mechanical errors in sentences that are otherwise correct in structure and content. Errors in spelling, punctuation, and capitalization can be corrected during the final "editing" process after the drafts of the essay are completed. However, do not give credit for fragments, run-on sentences, or sentences copied word for word from the reading. An acceptable topic sentence makes a declarative statement that correctly responds to the assignment; in this case, a topic sentence might be "The Tasaday had two useful stone tools."

After all the papers have been checked and the grades recorded, discuss the assignment with the class. Students who received "As" should read their sentences aloud while you write them on the board. This process shows the successful students that there can be more than one acceptable topic sentence; less-successful students can see what they should have done. Explain that every student who did not receive an "A" should choose one of the sentences on the board and copy it for use in completing his or her essay.

Step 3: Writing Major Supporting Detail Sentences. When every student has an acceptable topic sentence, the next task is to write two major supporting detail sentences. For this lesson, such a sentence might be "Their hammer ax was made from a smooth, egg-shaped stone." Again, go around the room and check papers as the students finish. Use the same criteria for judging these sentences that were used to evaluate the topic sentences. Debrief the activity as before. If a significant number of students do not succeed in this task, you might want to repeat this step after the unsuccessful students have had the opportunity to see the acceptable sentences.

Step 4: Writing Minor Supporting Detail Sentences. When each student has written two major supporting detail sentences, they can go on to write a minor supporting detail sentence that expands on the point made in each major sentence. For example, if a student's major detail sentence was "Their most important tool was a scraper, a small, flat, sharpened stone," an accompanying minor supporting detail sentence might be "The Tasaday used it for making digging sticks and knives out of bamboo." Follow the procedures used in steps 2 and 3 for evaluation and debriefing.

At this point each student should have a topic sentence and two pairs of major/minor supporting detail sentences. Pick two or three good examples of this combination and write them on the chalkboard in paragraph form. Allow some time for the students to copy their sentences in paragraph form.

Step 5: Writing a Conclusion. Ask each student to carefully read his or her paragraph and then write a one-sentence "conclusion." Point out that a good conclusion does not simply repeat the topic sentence. Suggest that an appropriate conclusion sentence might refer to the outcome of the events described in the paragraph. The opinion of the writer about the facts set forth in the paragraph might also be used as a conclusion. Some appropriate concluding sentences for a paragraph on this topic might be "These tools are just like tools people used in Stone Age times" and "The Tasaday got lots of work done with these simple tools." Evaluate and debrief the concluding sentences using the same procedures that were followed during earlier steps.

Step 6: Editing and Correcting. Each student now has a complete one- paragraph "mini-essay" on the topic of the Tasaday's stone tools. At this point the students need to correct any errors in spelling and punctuation. Allowing the students to exchange their papers with partners may help them identify errors. The corrected paragraphs should then be neatly copied in ink for final grading.

If the students seem ready to write at greater length, the activity can be expanded after step 5 by asking the students to copy the topic sentence, each major/minor detail sentence, and concluding sentence as four separate paragraphs. One or two additional supporting sentences can then be added to each paragraph. A fifth paragraph can be added by discussing a third tool. The possibilities for expanding this activity are limited only by the facts provided in the student reading. Not all steps need to be followed; the series could be ended at any point, depending on the needs of students and the amount of time available.

I like to use underlining lessons because they are short, they are easy to grade, and they serve several important educational goals. They also serve as an important springboard to a series of activities culminating in improved compositions.

17. AUTOBIOGRAPHICAL WRITING TO LEARN SOCIAL STUDIES

By James Willcock

One child sits quietly alone, contemplating her future. She is only 10 years old. Another tentatively tastes snake meat for the first time, discovering that he may like it after all. Elsewhere, two heads bend together, whispering conspiratorial plans for escape, as another mumbles to herself numbers representing a code that may lead to her freedom. All these children have either made their decisions or are about to make them; no matter what choices they make, they know that they will face hardships, the unknown, and possible death--just as they have throughout their lives as slaves.

These fifth-grade students are in the process of determining their futures as American slaves in the 1850s. They are participating in a social studies writing unit designed to give students a real sense of the lives of slaves, rather than just facts about slavery. During the previous four weeks, they have written about their lives in Africa, their capture, the sea voyage, their sale, their jobs, and their treatment and lives in America.

The basic purpose of the unit was to find an effective way of teaching slavery which included the experiences of slavery as well as the facts. It is important in this unit that students realize how blacks became increasingly separated from each other and from their African cultures, how they lost their rights and freedoms, how they lacked control over their own lives, and why some slaves accepted slavery while others fought back as best they could.

The autobiographical approach used in this unit involves each student in writing, as a series of seven successive chapters, what is in effect a book of his or her experiences as an African caught up in the slave trade and slavery. These chapters progress from life in Africa to the end of slavery.

Chapter 1: My Life in Africa

> My name is Tihana of the Yoruba tribe. I am 12 years old. My brothers are Bantha and Swaful and my mother's name is Maigho and my father's is Hiawja. We live in a small house of dry clay. It is warm here and it rains every day. When it rains there is lots of mud.--Jamie A.

The first chapter is both the most important and the least representative of the students' writing. Before writing, the students see filmstrips of the African rain forest and savanna, and then they discuss and compare what they have seen in each region--the land, animals, food, homes, and life styles. The filmstrips usually contain modern scenes, so the discussion seeks to draw out which things would or would not have been a part of the Africans' lives in the 1800s. Also, by seeing the filmstrips, the students get some idea of the range of the possible African life styles.

To prepare for writing the first chapter, each student rolls a die and, by the number cast, receives information on the life style, customs, and climate of either Ghana, the Senegalese region, the area of the Congo and Angola, or the Niger River region. Students then meet with others of the same area, read the information together, and divide as they wish into families, tribes, and clans to plan and write.

This chapter is important because the students need a good beginning to be able to write well throughout the unit. In groups they get necessary support, and they can discuss the material as much as they need to before writing. In this chapter their African characters take shape.

Unlike the emphasis in later chapters, the focus in this first chapter tends to be on facts. This type of writing is easier for students because they can organize these facts much as they would when writing a report. Later chapters require more imagination.

Chapter 2: The Capture

> My wife said that her mother and father turned into lovebirds when they disappeared. She said my mother and father turned into seagulls and flew away. I know this is her way of speaking of their disappearance without having to think of something bad happening to them.--Mark H.

A teacher preparing this unit needs to do quite a bit of research to find materials that will bring the slave experience to life for the students. In every succeeding chapter, students begin to assimilate new information into their writing. In the excerpt above, Mark uses African beliefs in animism (belief that spirits exist in plants and animals), taken from his first chapter, to explain the disappearance of people into slavery.

Students enjoy doing the second chapter because it involves action writing. There is potential for suspense in writing about how Africans changed their ways of life and their laws because of the slave trade by either becoming warlike, cowering in their huts at night, ceasing to farm in order to concentrate on defense, or even becoming slavers themselves. The action writing comes in describing their capture, and writing about feelings is required in describing the misery of the march to the sea and imprisonment. This chapter requires more imagination than the first, but it is an easy type of creativity for students because it involves action rather than character development. This chapter is enhanced by showing pictures and drawings of slave forts, types of restraints, and slaves in chains; such pictures can be found in many resource books.

Chapter 3: The Slave Ship

> They led us over to a pole and chained us to it. Then they took a large iron out and put it into the fire until it became red. They said something, but I couldn't understand what they were saying. They took the iron and pressed it on Tattoo's shoulder. Tattoo yelled with paid until one of them took out a whip. Then they came to me. I tried desperately to get away, but the chains were too strong. They pressed it on my shoulder. I tried to yell, but the pain was too great. It was like putting your shoulder in the fire.--Chris M.

The horror and misery of the slave ship is the most commonly found type of slave information. One excellent selection from Rum, Slaves, and Molasses, by Clifford L. Alderman (New York: Crowell-Collier, 1972), is a good introduction to read to the students. This chapter requires yet another type of writing--descriptive, personal accounts of slaves as being essentially alone in their misery, yet aware of misery all around them.

In working on this chapter, students should share what they are writing, either in small groups or with the whole class. This is a pivotal chapter because the students move from story writing into personal narrative, where their feelings and actions are the most important aspect. By sharing, students get support for this type of writing and feel more comfortable expressing feelings or writing detailed descriptions. Collecting and reproducing the strongest passages for class distribution is a good idea before students rewrite their drafts, since these good examples can be used as models.

Chapter 4: The Auction

> We walked a long time and then we reached a thing with boards nailed together. About a hundred people were standing there. Some white man pushed me up onto it. My knees were shaking like I had knobby knees, and then some men started yelling something in some weird language. Some man came and grabbed me like I was a banana or something. He took me somewhere, but I am not sure where at all.--Laura B.

By now the pattern of introducing information and then discussing it before writing has been well established. At this point the students can be given information about how and where the slaves were sold. The discussion that follows can center on what an African might understand of the auction process and what it would be like. Students then write about the experience of being auctioned. Midway through their writing, before they get to the point of being sold, each one stops and rolls a die twice. The die in this unit represents the uncertainty of a slave's life; the two rolls determine to which of 11 different states each slave will be taken. (The meanings of the numbers should be withheld until the following chapter.) The students suddenly realize that they are being separated from one another. Until now, all the students in the class have shared the same experiences since leaving Africa. Now, they discover that they are being separated, but they are not yet sure where they are going. This chapter evokes more-personal narratives because it lacks the mass of descriptive facts used in the slave ship chapter. The students must create more of the sense of the auction in their minds.

Even-more-effective writing occurs if this scene can be dramatized. A colleague led her students in a simple but very effective play depicting an auction in progress. The lights then went out and a spotlight was placed on each cast member, who answered questions posed first by "newspaper reporters" (also cast members) and then by the audience. The writing done after this play was personal, descriptive, detailed, and effective.

Chapter 5: My Job

> Suddenly, in an instant, I heard a whip cracking. I looked up and there was the same man. He threw me some old rags. I didn't know why he threw me those rags, but then I realized he wanted me to put them on. Then he gave me wooden shoes. When I stood up, they hurt my feet. The man pointed but I didn't know where, so I just followed everyone else. Then I wondered what to do. I saw what they were doing, they were looking for rock-like plants. I wasn't very good at it at first, but I got used to it. The day seemed never to end.--Mike W.

Before the students write chapter 5, the teacher distributes handouts containing information (from encyclopedias) about the climate, working conditions, and methods of growing crops in 11 southern states. Before writing, the students again roll the die. The lucky ones who roll one certain number become house slaves; the rest work the fields. With this chapter, the emphasis returns to description and facts because of the thousands of possibilities for jobs, treatment, and living conditions.

Chapter 6: My Life as a Slave

> As the days went by, I saw some of my friends being sold down the river. It scared me that maybe I would one day be sold down the river. Then, yesterday I met up with a house slave. We gave each other dirty looks. At first I was scared and then said to myself, "Why?" I almost started a fight then, but my overseer came by and I left quickly.--Karen B.

A roll of the die provides students with information for this chapter. The first type of information deals with treatment. Actual quotations from such books as In Their Own Words and To Be a Slave (see list of resources at end of chapter) can be used to provide this information.

Another roll of the die provides access to information on such attitudes or activities as being hired out to work, going to a slave breaker, being married, attending a jubilee, singing songs and learning their meanings, learning how to act around the slavemaster, the interaction between house and field slaves, bad times and the selling of friends or family, and dealing with fears, slave codes, and family life. Students can incorporate this information into their characters' lives. It is with this chapter and the next that sharing of writing again becomes essential because of the wealth of information about slave life that is scattered throughout the classroom. Experience indicates, however, that by now students are already sharing the information anyway.

Chapter 7: The End

> One day I was sitting down to rest my bones and I heard someone singing. I looked over and it was a white man studying the birds. He told me about the Underground Railroad and taught me the codes.--Suzie M.
>
> After I was sold to a plantation in Kentucky, I was made a house slave. One day our master came to talk to us. He said, "Congratulations, I hear you both are getting married." Then we both exclaimed, "What?" "Yep, you are getting married, I just arranged it."--Indra K.

This final chapter requires considerable preparation through discussions that follow the showing of filmstrips on Nat Turner's rebellion and on Harriet Tubman and the Underground Railroad, information sheets on the slaves' perceptions of escape taken from the writings of Frederick Douglass, and readings about the perils of escape, including slave codes, patrols, catchers, and the Fugitive Slave Law. A selection from *Rum, Slaves, and Molasses* describes runaways in the swamps and their life there. Constructing a student-generated list of a slave's alternatives, along with the advantages and perils of each choice, is helpful at this point.

The students can then choose what they wish to do with their lives--stay on the plantation, run away, or rebel. After choosing, each rolls a die to find out the consequences of his or her choice.

Those who rebel have a very slight chance of success and a very good chance of dying. The information they receive basically involves how they might organize a rebellion, how it might proceed, and the outcome.

Those who choose to run away roll a die to find out whether they will go on their own or with the aid of the Underground Railroad. Information about the Underground Railroad includes data about prominent conductors and their methods and routes. For instance, Harriet Tubman, following East Coast routes, had several narrow escapes. Calvin Fairbanks in the central regions used many disguises, and Alexander Ross in the West taught slaves a code to use. For those on the Underground Railroad, a final roll of the die gives a conclusion which might include recapture, escape and a job in a northern city, escape to Canada, near recapture, or even recapture years later under the Fugitive Slave Law.

For those running away alone, a roll of the die determines whether they will be recaptured, join up with the Underground Railroad somewhere, find refuge in the swamps or with Indian tribes, successfully escape only to be kidnapped later, or escape completely.

Those who stay face either division of their families, no change at all, the Civil War, being resold, repatriation in Liberia, or any number of other personal choices.

Teaching this type of unit effectively requires quite a bit of preparation and research. The students need background material to read before writing every chapter, and the later chapters require a wide variety of information. Most of this information can be secured from any adequate school library. The sources listed at the end of this chapter, along with encyclopedias, can provide all the information needed in teaching this unit. Although the volume of initial work is great, the material is not consumed by the students, and it can be reused and added to in future years. A file of pictures and drawings can also be built over time to help the students visualize the situations about which they write. Approximately one month is required for writing, discussion, revision, and sharing of written work.

During this unit, student writing proceeds from report writing, in which facts are merely reorganized and restated (as in chapters 1 and 5), to creative story writing and descriptive writing (chapters 2 and 3), to a personal narrative, resembling a diary or journal (chapters 6 and 7). It is important to allow sufficient time for sharing and revising--especially in the third and final two chapters, when the emphasis is on personal feelings and a large variety of information. This sharing process improves writing by stimulating students to write their best; it also gives students models of good writing to emulate. However, the value of this type of writing unit lies in the development not only of the students' writing skills but also of their understanding of the myriad facets of the slave experience. Sequential autobiographical writing can help students learn history as well as improve their ability to write.

Resources for Students

Alderman, Clifford L. Rum, Slaves, and Molasses. New York: Crowell-Collier, 1972. (Follows the actual voyage of a 19th-century slaver, with excellent descriptions of the slave coast, ship conditions, and New World markets.)

Buckmaster, Henrietta. Flight to Freedom. New York: Thomas Y. Crowell, 1955. (Stories of the Underground Railroad, routes, people, techniques, and history.)

David, Daniel S. Struggle for Freedom. New York: Harcourt Brace Jovanovich, 1972. (Study of abolitionist movements with some discussion of slave conditions.)

Douglass, Frederick. Narrative of the Life of Frederick Douglass. New York: Doubleday, 1963. (Descriptive first-hand passages of life as a slave; excellent source of information on treatment.)

Everett, Susanne. The Slaves. New York: G.P. Putnam's Sons, 1978. (Bountifully illustrated book with photographs depicting every aspect of slave life from the capture on.)

Hughes, Langston, and Milton Meltzer. A Pictorial History of the Negro in America. New York: Crown, 1963. (Fully illustrated subject-by-subject review of all aspects of black life in America, including free blacks and the era after slavery.)

Ingraham, Leonard W. Slavery in the United States. New York: Franklin Watts, 1968. (Easy-to-read description of plantation life and rebellions, with good line drawings about slave life.)

Katz, William L. Slavery to the Civil War, 1812-1865. New York: Franklin Watts, 1974. (Much like Slavery in the United States in scope and subject matter, but concentrates more on history than on slave life.)

Lester, Julius. To Be a Slave. New York: Dial, 1968. (Collection of quotations from slaves on every aspect of their lives.)

Meltzer, Milton. In Their Own Words, 1619-1865. New York: Thomas Y. Crowell, 1965. (Collection of slave quotations describing every aspect of their lives and treatment.)

In addition to the above books, a number of filmstrips can be used in teaching this unit. Encyclopaedia Brittanica produces two sets of relevant filmstrips, A People Uprooted, 1500-1800 (five filmstrips tracing the African experience through the slave trade to slavery in America) and Chains of Slavery, 1800-1865 (five filmstrips on various black leaders and the black experience in America in the period before the Civil War). McGraw-Hill produces three filmstrips: one on the African slave trade and two on slavery in America. A critical-thinking filmstrip, Triangular Trade Route, by Modern Learning Aids, can be very useful in stimulating thinking in this unit.

IV. COMBINING WRITING WITH SOCIAL STUDIES

Merely using the techniques suggested in Parts II and III will not go very far toward improving either student writing or subject-matter learning in elementary school social studies. If we really wish to achieve these two goals for most of our students, we must go further. At least three specific conditions are required, in addition to knowledge and use of effective classroom techniques, in order to successfully integrate instruction in writing and social studies content in the elementary school classroom.

First, as Nellie Quander points out in Chapter 18, teachers cannot effectively use these techniques without due regard for the basic factors that make for good classroom lessons. Quander writes as an experienced elementary teacher and principal and past president of the National Association of Elementary School Principals. Her concern is with the quality of classroom learning and with students and their needs as well as with lessons that have maximum meaning and purpose for students. The considerations and guidelines outlined by Quander underscore what teachers and students need to know and do if the techniques presented in Parts II and III are to be productive in actual classroom use.

Second, in order to successfully teach writing in elementary school social studies, classroom teachers need certain kinds of support. Language-arts curriculum specialist Betty Blaisdell and social studies specialist Barry K. Beyer describe three essential supports in Chapter 19--a detailed curriculum guide, inservice teacher training, and cooperative teacher/administrator assessment procedures.

Finally, effective writing instruction in elementary school social studies must be part of a coherent, systematic, developmental program of studies. As Barry K. Beyer points out in Chapter 20, such a program has three essential features: sequential development of specific writing skills, careful integration of writing with social studies instruction, and provision for direct skill instruction throughout the program. The ideal elementary school social studies/writing curriculum is one that helps students in each grade level reinforce skills learned in preceding grades while developing new skills needed to carry out tasks that will be introduced in subsequent grades, all in the context of content appropriate to the specific grade and subject. What students write about--the content they use and the ideas they seek to communicate and develop--is as important in social studies teaching as how they go about their writing. Effective integration of writing and social studies requires attention to substance as well as to technique. The final chapter in the book outlines and illustrates the basic substantive elements of an effective elementary school social studies writing program.

That integrating instruction and practice in writing with elementary school social studies content can be done--and is being done--is illustrated by the articles presented in this book. Yet much remains to be done if we are to realize the full potential of this approach to skill and subject-matter teaching. The three chapters that follow outline the most important factors that must be considered and some steps that must be taken in order to realize the full benefit of the techniques described in Parts II and III.

18. BUILDING EFFECTIVE WRITING LESSONS

By Nellie Quander

Teachers often ask for new ideas that can be used in their classrooms. It is sometimes a status symbol to be the first on a staff to bring a new idea into the school. But a lesson, to be educationally sound, must consist of more than the use of new techniques or materials. A teacher must be sure that a lesson meets the needs of the students, incorporates sound principles of learning, and achieves the school's curriculum goals before introducing it into the classroom.

How can a teacher determine a lesson's soundness? As a principal, I usually suggested nine criteria that should be met in order to have a top-notch lesson. These criteria may be helpful to teachers who wish to use in their classrooms the ideas and techniques presented in this book.

<u>Criterion 1: The Lesson Should Build on Students' Experiences</u>. We know that learning and experience are closely interrelated. Experiences of many kinds provide a basis on which new concepts can be built and new skills broadened or developed. Children who have lived on a farm, in the inner city, in suburbia, at the seaside, in a desert, or in the mountains have probably all shared some common experiences. We might guess that most have watched television, eaten cereal for breakfast, and ridden or at least seen a bicycle. We can also assume that children living in each of these varied places have had experiences that may not be known to or understood by other children in this vast group. Even children living in fairly close proximity to one another may have significant differences in their past experiences. These experiences influence the students' perceptions of new information and experiences.

In planning a lesson, a teacher must ask, "What experiences have my students had that I might use to help them understand this activity?" It is difficult to forget the panic that engulfed me during my very first week of teaching. I had spent a significant amount of time studying the teacher's guide and preparing the reading lesson. The first question I was directed to ask was, "How many of you have ever been on a train ride?" When only two of the children raised their hands, I was shocked. I certainly could not ask the second question, which was, "How many of you remember the man who took your ticket?" Somehow, I recovered quickly enough to arrange a simulated train ride in the classroom before proceeding with the lesson. I learned a valuable lesson during that first week of teaching: my students' past experiences were critically important when a new idea was introduced.

Sometimes teachers assume that many of their students' experiences have no value in new learning, and they fail to use these experiences to help children understand a new idea. For example, many young children in poor areas have had extensive experience in handling money. They may be sent to the store several times in one day. They cross busy streets, read labels on packages, and count change accurately. Their teachers are often unaware of the valuable nature of these experiences as they proceed to cut out pictures of rabbits in an attempt to teach counting. Teachers need to build on the experiences of their students. This is especially true in teaching writing--in elementary school social studies or in any other subject area.

Teachers especially need to use students' experiences as the basis of written work when students are just beginning to learn the writing process. The reason is simple: learning basic writing skills involves considerable abstraction. When students begin writing, they should not have to deal simultaneously with strange new skills and new content. If students write about content with which they are already familiar, they can concentrate on learning a new skill. But trying to deal with new content unrelated to their prior experiences as well as with new and rather abstract skills often proves to be too much for beginning writers.

Criterion 2: The Lesson Should Be Related to Students' Interests. It is easier to teach something new when the interests or preferences of the learner are considered. Students usually have a broad range of interests, and a teacher should make every effort to discover these interests in order to use them in learning activities. If sports, animals, television programs, comic strips, toys, fashions, automobiles, detectives, food, and Space Invaders are of major interest to students, teachers should work these topics into lessons from time to time.

On one occasion when I visited a classroom I noticed that several children in the group were not paying attention when the teacher introduced a new topic. When I talked with the teacher afterward, he said, "Well, there are always a few who don't pay attention. I will send their parents letters immediately to warn them of the consequences of the children's inattentive behavior." I suggested that before letters were sent to parents we should examine the lesson to see whether changes in the presentation might change student behavior. When we examined the lesson, we agreed that the students might have paid more attention if the examples used by the teacher had reflected topics of more interest to the students. Within a few minutes, the teacher and I came up with seven or eight ways that topics of interest to the students could be included in the introduction of the lesson and the examples. Two weeks later, the teacher told me, "I don't know how I could have overlooked such an obvious technique, but it really helps to use the students' concerns. Come to visit again soon and observe for yourself the change that has taken place."

Using material of interest to students is one way of getting their attention, but it has additional rewards. When a teacher is sufficiently concerned to discover topics of interest to students and use those topics in the presentation of a lesson, a feeling of caring is transmitted to students. The feeling that the teacher really cares often seems to make a difference in student behavior. This caring feeling is an important part of a classroom climate that supports and encourages young children as they begin to write.

Writing based on students' interests differs from experience-based writing in that the former utilizes or reflects what students like or prefer, whether or not it is part of their past experience. Students may be interested in prehistoric animals, for example. Their interest may or may not have led them to museums or books where they could see renderings of such animals or to watch movies that depicted these creatures--all forms of experience. Even without such experiences, many children can conjure up images of how prehistoric animals looked, behaved, or even felt! They can write about these imagined creatures.

Since writing is an intensely personal act, it requires a trusting, nonthreatening classroom climate. Lessons that reflect students' interests help create and maintain the kind of classroom climate in which student writing can flourish. Moreover, students write more easily and their writing flows more smoothly if what they write about is tied to a particular interest of the class or of individual children.

Criterion 3: The Lesson Should Include Strategies for Motivating Students to Participate. When a teacher reviews the curriculum for the year, it is easy to spot concepts or skills that must be taught but which have never been special favorites of the majority of the students. During this initial review of curriculum, the teacher should begin to consider strategies for motivating students' interest in achieving these goals. The more abstract the concept or skill, the more elaborate the motivational device should be. Many children need something special to arouse their interest in topics presented to them. Students often do not see a need to learn about Stone Age people, or their own community, or America's past. The skillful teacher, however, can make a difference by presenting new content or skill lessons in ways that motivate interest.

Once, while observing a fifth-grade classroom, I noticed that the teacher introduced a social studies unit by saying, "This is difficult, but all boys and girls must learn this information before they can be promoted to the sixth grade." In the classroom next door, the teacher approached the unit by announcing, "In about 20 minutes all of you will be able to answer questions about this topic that no one can answer now. You will be so proud of yourselves that you will hardly be able to wait to find out more about this tomorrow." Each teacher used a motivation strategy, but which teacher probably got the best results?

Obviously, the second approach encouraged the children to become involved in the lesson. They were anxious to go on to the next day. Learners enjoy the challenge of solving a mystery or making a discovery or winning a game or knowing something that others don't know, and motivational techniques that appeal to learners in these ways can inspire participation.

When my own children were in elementary school, they asked me several times to buy the newest cereal on the market. I reminded them of our rule: "If I buy it, you must eat it." On this particular occasion the cereal was awful, and they begged me to relax the rule. At that time I was an elementary school teacher, and I was curious to learn how they had been convinced that they wanted that cereal. They told me that it had been advertised on television. I began to watch commercials, particularly those directed at children. I concluded that Madison Avenue had done its homework and knew how to appeal to children. I decided that if a television commercial could sell that awful cereal to my children, I ought to be able to sell any item in the public school curriculum. Since that time I have pointed out to teachers that they might do well to borrow the motivational techniques used in children's commercials as strategies for selling their lessons.

Motivation is an important part of effective instruction. Examining objects from an old trunk, questioning one's grandparents, creating fantasy field trips--all these activities serve as effective motivators for writing instruction and practice. Not only do these experiences help students become quickly involved in the writing process, they also provide a meaningful context in which writing can take place. Effective motivation doesn't merely draw students into learning; it also provides a purpose for learning which carries students through the entire experience.

Criterion 4: The Lesson Should Take Into Account Knowledge About Developmental Learning. We know that most children learn through a developmental or cumulative process. They learn step 1, step 2, step 3, and so on. Although most teachers seem to be aware of the cumulative nature of learning, teaching does not always reflect this understanding. Students at any level are frustrated when they are unable to connect what is presented to them with what they already know. Thus, choosing and conducting lessons requires critical professional judgments that should be based on intimate knowledge of the developmental stages of students, in every subject area and at all levels of learning.

Moreover, teachers are sometimes driven by the desire to cover a certain amount of material, to follow the curriculum for a certain grade, or merely to provide a lesson appropriate for a particular time period. It may be that a day of review should precede the presentation of new material. Teachers cannot assume that students remember things from last year, last month--or, in some cases, last week or even yesterday.

Nor can teachers afford to overlook the red flags that students wave to indicate that there is a problem. When many students are confused, the problem cannot be assumed to be inattentive behavior. Teachers must listen carefully to students' comments, observe their facial expressions, consider reluctance to respond, and observe common errors on completed tasks in determining whether the lesson being presented is appropriate for students and within their grasp.

This caution is especially important in writing instruction. We simply cannot assume that students know how to do what we want them to do. Teachers need to provide direct instruction in each skill that constitutes the writing process. For best results, as Janet Cuenca notes (see Chapter 16), they need to do so in "small bites." The writing skills being taught need to be broken into small parts, each of which builds from the preceding one to the next. Students need to be explicitly taught how to do each step, and they need repeated opportunities to practice each step under supervision before trying the next step. Teachers need to demonstrate the various skills as well as explain them and to provide group instruction before sending students off to work alone.

For example, children should be given an opportunity to contribute to a collectively created sentence, paragraph, or letter before they make their own attempts at these forms of writing. By doing this they can learn the correct form, the kind of information that can be included, and the ways in which it can be arranged. Then, working in pairs, students can repeat the process and share the results. Only after they have received the kind of guidance provided by such cooperative activities can students be expected to work alone with confidence.

The exact developmental sequence for learning to write may yet be in dispute; however, the idea of breaking the overall process into sequential steps, to be introduced and reinforced slowly over time, makes sense in terms of developmental learning. The vast majority of children need careful, repeated, specific instruction in order to develop skills and ideas effectively.

<u>Criterion 5: The Lesson Should Proceed From the Concrete to the Abstract</u>. Most teachers understand the need to present ideas with concrete objects or illustrations. Yet too often this step is missing when a skill lesson is taught. Skills that teachers understand from years of experience usually are new to their students. It is necessary to begin with the simplest possible illustration and to add details as the skill is practiced. Thus, in introducing any complex writing task, the best results will occur when it is gradually introduced in terms of concrete examples and experiential learning activities.

The use of such content and experiences is extremely important in teaching writing to beginning students in elementary school social studies. The "old trunk in the attic" (see Chapter 8) approach is one example of a concrete learning experience that is useful in introducing writing. Making and using word caches or word banks (Chapter 10) is another. Providing examples of letters that other students have written before asking students to write their own is yet another (see Chapter 13). The importance of providing an array of specific examples before presenting an abstract idea or a new skill cannot be stressed enough.

Criterion 6: The Lesson Should Actively Involve Students. As the steps of a lesson are put together, the teacher should consider ways in which students might participate in each step. In some lessons it might be useful to engage students in the introduction; in other lessons it might be best for students to develop examples; in still other lessons the students might be expected to provide conclusions. Many lessons will present the opportunity to involve students in every step. The point is that teachers must be aware of the need to provide students with opportunities to participate.

Involvement is one way of giving students "ownership" of the lesson. When students are actively involved, they pay attention and realize the value of their contributions. They understand that they have something to offer, and they look forward to participating in the next lesson. Successful participation allows students to take risks and to go beyond what is required. Perhaps more important, involvement in an activity helps students remember the lesson.

However, sometimes it is easy to confuse involvement in a lesson with the completion of an assignment. The teacher introduces the lesson, lectures, provides examples, and makes an assignment. The teacher considers the final assignment "involvement," when in fact the lesson is over and students have played no active part. Whether or not the assignment is graded, what the teacher has essentially done is give a test on the lecture.

Active student involvement is especially important in skill learning. Writing is an extremely active process that requires social as well as physical and intellectual activity on the part of every student. Such prewriting activities as brainstorming and building word caches, which involve students actively, not only lead to the invention of something worth writing about but also stimulate creative thinking in students. The processes of sharing what has been written, participating in peer reviews or peer editing, and compiling written work into booklets also actively involve students and thus promote a sense of creative ownership which sparks learning and skill mastery.

Criterion 7: The Lesson Should Take Into Account Variations in Learning Styles. Although more research on learning styles is needed, we do know some things about learning styles. First, students use all five senses to learn. Second, some learners grasp new ideas quickly, while others need repeated lessons.

Many lessons are designed to appeal to the visual learner. In fact, many teachers assign most lessons as reading assignments: "Read pages 37 and 38 and answer the questions on page 39." Students who are visual learners can be expected to do well with this type of lesson. When the teacher spends 90 percent of the class time talking, the auditory learners can be expected to learn faster. But what happens to the children who learn best when they have an opportunity to both see and hear what is being taught?

In early elementary school grades, teachers seem to give their students many opportunities to see, hear, touch, taste, and smell. As the students progress, many teachers feel that opportunities to use senses other than sight and hearing are not needed.

In writing in social studies, teachers need to create lessons that use visual as well as written stimuli, oral as well as written composing, and peer as well as individual feedback or evaluation. Opportunities for group as well as individual practice should be built into lessons. Differentiated assignments, such as those used in creating fantasy field trips (see Chapter 14), allow for varied learning styles as well as varied interests and abilities. When a lesson is designed to appeal to only one style of learning, it is safe to assume that many learners have been excluded. If a new concept is presented with several learning styles in mind and repeated with slight variations, many students will have an opportunity to learn the new idea.

Criterion 8: The Lesson Should Provide Opportunities for Practice. When new skills are learned, they must be practiced. Not even the best possible teaching techniques will ensure that students will retain what they have learned if they are not given adequate opportunity to practice.

Provision for practice should not be haphazard; practice must be planned. When students have learned a skill and the teacher moves on to another skill, seat work must include opportunities to practice what has been learned. Often, when teachers speak of students who have "free time" in the classroom, they mean <u>undirected</u> time. When some students have completed an activity and are waiting for others to finish, that time can be used for planned practice.

Teachers should not be reluctant to provide repeated opportunities for practice, especially in writing. For example, students can practice punctuation skills by punctuating dittoed, unpunctuated paragraphs from a text or other source as they review a social studies lesson and by reviewing and revising the punctuation of other students' paragraphs. Similar kinds of practice opportunities can be used in teaching most writing skills. The value of such practice should not be underestimated; however, it must be purposeful rather than just drill for the sake of drill. Teachers need to constantly remind themselves that practice for which students see no purpose turns them off and may well inhibit skill learning.

Furthermore, mastery of a few skills is much more important than superficial understanding of many, especially for beginning writers. Teachers too often confuse quantity with quality. It is much more important for students to produce one really good sentence or paragraph than to write a dozen sentences or paragraphs merely for display. Practice--well planned and reinforced with instruction where appropriate--is a vital part of the learning process in writing, as it is in other skills and knowledge areas.

<u>Criterion 9: The Lesson Should Have Purpose and Meaning</u>. Students should be given many opportunities to use what they have learned in meaningful ways. Every time I observed one teacher's six-day process for teaching spelling, I cringed. The spelling words were introduced on Monday, examined on Tuesday, pretested on Wednesday, reviewed on Thursday, tested on Friday--and forgotten on Saturday, rarely to be seen or heard again that year. New knowledge and skills are not retained unless students are provided with meaningful ways to use what they have learned. Just as practice must be planned, however, opportunities to use new skills must be planned. What have we accomplished if we teach students all the rules of punctuation but provide few opportunities for those rules to be used? What difference will it make if our students remember accurately the definitions of 300 words, if they have no opportunity to use those words in speaking, reading, and writing?

Writing in elementary school social studies in order to learn about social studies topics or skills gives meaning and purpose to writing. Such writing is not simply an exercise. Writing a script for a simulated field trip, writing a poem for an "ABC" book, writing a chapter for a larger story, writing a letter to request information--all are meaningful uses of writing for content purposes. In addition to teaching new skills and thought processes, writing activities can reinforce what students have learned as well as help them invent, use, explore, and evaluate new information and ideas. When writing is used to accomplish such content-related goals, it becomes a purposeful and meaningful activity.

This book presents sample lessons that will help teachers improve student writing and their learning of social studies skills and knowledge. However, in order to be most effective, these sample lessons must be adapted to meet the needs of students in any particular classroom. If this adaptation process takes into consideration the nine criteria presented here, we can be sure that our efforts to use writing in elementary school social studies will result in the highest quality possible in the teaching/learning process.

19. KEYS TO A SUCCESSFUL SOCIAL STUDIES WRITING PROGRAM

By Betty Jefferson Blaisdell and Barry K. Beyer

What is required for a successful writing program in elementary school social studies? That question brings to mind a conversation between Humpty Dumpty and Alice in Lewis Carroll's Through the Looking Glass*:

> "When *I* use a word," Humpty Dumpty said, in rather a scornful tone, "it means just what I choose it to mean--neither more nor less."
>
> "The question is," said Alice, "whether you *can* make words mean so many different things."
>
> "The question is," said Humpty Dumpty, "which is to be master--that's all."

The teacher is the master of any successful writing program. Given appropriate support, classroom teachers determine the success of writing programs in elementary school social studies and, for that matter, in other content areas as well.

To have a chance for success, however, even the most committed teachers need the support of a carefully articulated curriculum guide, an effective staff-development program, and a cooperative teacher/administrator assessment plan. Each dimension depends on the other. The curriculum guide serves as a foundation for the program. It defines and describes the writing program. It also ensures continuity in learning, with writing objectives for students specified at each grade level. Such a guide is of little use, however, if teachers are not given the opportunity and time to explore their own teaching strengths and ideas in conjunction with the curriculum guide. A staff-development program that assists teachers in implementing the writing program as defined in the curriculum guide provides the link between the guide and classroom application. Administrators who support the teachers in their endeavors

---

*Reprinted with permission from Alice's Adventures in Wonderland and Through the Looking Glass, by Lewis Carroll (New York: Collier Books, a division of Macmillan Publishing Co., Inc.; London: Collier Macmillan Publishers, 1962). Copyright 1962 by Macmillan Publishing Co., Inc.

to improve student writing and who cooperatively plan an assessment program with the teachers provide the final support for a successful subject-matter writing program.

Curriculum Guide

A carefully structured and detailed curriculum guide is indisputably an important key to the successful teaching of writing in elementary school social studies. This guide should be written by experienced teachers representing different grade levels and should contain five basic components.

First, such a guide should present a philosophy that articulates the importance of writing and the importance of teaching writing. This philosophy could well be built around the importance of writing for discovering ideas, for organizing information, and for learning content, much as is done in the prologue to this book.

Second, the guide needs to clarify the nature of writing as done by beginners. Student growth in writing occurs gradually. Students develop best in classrooms where teachers provide many opportunities for practicing and experimenting with a variety of writing activities for a wide range or purposes--to organize ideas, to express opinions, to explore feelings, to remember information, or to inform or persuade someone.

As part of this description of writing, the curriculum guide should outline the basic aspects of the writing process. A three- or four-stage process for teaching writing can be an effective model for teaching students how to organize their thinking and communicate meaning clearly to others. Prewriting, composing, and postwriting are the three basic stages of the writing process; a fourth stage, sharing, is sometimes added as well. By using this process when teaching students to write, we provide them with a framework that they can use as they grow into independent writers.

Prewriting activities help students identify their audience and understand the purpose of the particular writing task. These preliminary activities stimulate students to generate, expand, and focus ideas. Composing activities provide students with practice in organizing their ideas into written form. Postwriting activities help students refine and revise their writing. Sharing activities allow students to develop a sense of competency and a delight in their ability to write. The stages of the writing process do not necessarily follow a consecutive order; they are recursive in nature. For example, sharing and revision may occur during the composing stage, composing activities may begin during the prewriting stage, or the prewriting activities of generating and expanding ideas may extend into the composing and postwriting stages.

Third, to be most useful to teachers, a guide should delineate the specific writing skills and concepts to be practiced at each level of student learning. At each level these skills should be sequentially developed and should build on and reinforce skills from preceding levels. For example, at the primary level, students may practice sentence development in kindergarten by dictating one or more sentences that describe pictures or objects; in grade 1 they may write sentences in response to a simple question; in grades 2 and 3 they may write sentences that describe events or persons. At the upper-elementary level, students may practice paragraph development in grade 4 by writing four or five sentences to support a given topic sentence; in grade 5, they can write paragraphs that contain a topic sentence, several supporting sentences, and a concluding sentence; and, finally, sixth-graders can be expected to write effective paragraphs which include interesting sentences that vary in style and pattern.

It is important that students have ample opportunities for translating their thinking into clearly written expression. It is equally important that students have guidance in learning how to write effectively. Teachers need to provide instruction for students in developing and expressing ideas as well as in using the conventions of edited American English. In fact, teaching the conventions of edited American English should be done primarily during the writing process and only secondarily through related exercises. The most significant instruction in writing should concentrate on generating, developing, and organizing ideas effectively. Writing clear sentences and adhering to correct usage are next in importance. Choosing the best words to get across the intended meaning and using correct spelling, punctuation, capitalization, indentations, and margins, as well as legible handwriting, are necessary to produce a polished paper.

Fourth, in addition to identifying specific skills, a useful guide should identify the different forms that writing can take; for example, class notes, letters, reports, journals, diaries, personal essays, stories, poems, and scripts. Teachers can introduce and teach these forms at specified grades, and students can continue to practice them in subsequent grades. For example, to ensure a variety of writing experiences during the elementary grades, the guide might sequence these writing forms as shown in Figure 6.

Finally, the guide should suggest writing activities that require students to write for different reasons. Students learn to use a variety of words and writing skills when they write for different purposes and audiences. The skills used to transmit information, explanations, or instructions differ from those used to persuade or to express an opinion. When students record facts, they use and practice writing skills different from those used to express personal feelings. Different audiences also require different approaches. When students write persuasive letters to classmates, they use more-informal language and possibly a different kind of reasoning than they would use with the editor of the local newspaper.

To help students develop varied syntactic skills, teachers need to use a variety of writing activities. With guidance from the teacher, students may undertake the following projects:[1]

--Writing and illustrating stories or making books about themselves for self-awareness units.

--Writing thank-you letters after a field trip or following a visit by a community resource person.

--Studying pictures of historical scenes and then pretending to be objects in the pictures. (Discuss what historical event the object may have witnessed and the circumstances which led up to the event. Write a lively account of the event portrayed in the picture as though the object is telling the story. As an alternative, select two objects in the picture and make up a conversation they might have about the historical event and its significance. Share orally with classmates or dramatize the event.)

--Interviewing family members to collect information about life during their childhood. (Write a list of questions before the interview and record the answers during or after the interview. In written form, compare and contrast the customs, clothing, transportation, and communication systems of today with those of earlier times. Compile the information into a class publication.)

Figure 6

FORMS OF WRITING IN THE ELEMENTARY GRADES*

Children should experience a variety of expository, narrative, and poetic writing in the elementary grades. Beginning in kindergarten and first grade, students dictate sentences and simple stories, which are written down by someone else. Toward the end of the first grade, students may work in groups to write simple stories and copy class-written letters. The forms listed below can be introduced between grade 2 and grade 6. After a form has been mastered, students should continue to practice it in subsequent grades.

Expository		Narrative		Poetic	
Form	Grade	Form	Grade	Form	Grade
Personal experiences	2	Plays		Poems	
Letters		Script dialogue	3	Cinquain	3
Invitation	2	Dialogue for an episode	4	Rhymed verse	3
Friendly	2	Script for skit	6	Concrete	3
Thank-you	4	Stories		Patterned	4
Social note	5	Simple story	2	Haiku	5
Business	5	Fable	4	Limerick	5
Reports		Myth	4	Diamanté	6
Chronological	2	Tall tale	4	Free verse	6
Simple report	3	Folktale	5	Acrostics	4
Short report on given topic	4	Adventure	5		
Notes	4	Fantasy	5		
Bibliography	4	Legend	6		
Diary	4	Heroic adventure	6		
Journal	4	Science fiction	6		
Book report	5	Personal experience	6		
News report	5				
Cutline	5				
Biography	5				
Autobiography	6				
Feature article	6				
Interview	6				
Application (for job)	6				
Directions					
Two-step	2				
Location	5				
Commercials					
Radio or TV	5				
Slogan or jingle	5				
Paragraphs					
Explanatory	3				
Ending for a story	3				
Descriptive	4				
Sequential	4				
Anecdotal	5				
Persuasive	6				

*Reprinted by permission from Guide for Teaching Writing, K-6, in the Fairfax County Public Schools, Part 1 (Fairfax, Va.: Fairfax County Public Schools, 1970).

--Tracing an imaginary journey on a map from a given departure point to a specific destination. (Keep a journal during the "trip," describing places visited along the way.)

--Pretending to be early settlers in America and writing letters to friends to persuade them to emigrate to America.

--Writing biographies or stories of imaginary colonial children. (Include as much factual information as possible about events, ways of living, and real people who made history.)

--Practicing giving precise directions--first orally, then in writing. (Practice how to give directions to school visitors to help them go from the classroom to other places in the school. Use a community map with cardinal and intermediate directions to practice giving precise oral and written directions for going from home or school to other places in the community.)

--Taking notes during media presentations and using them as sources of information for class discussion or for writing paragraphs or reports.

--Writing progress reports on projects. (Indicate when the project was begun, what steps are necessary to complete the task, and when the project will be completed.)

--Discussing current events and issues and then writing persuasive statements of positions on issues that currently face school children. (During the study of history, identify issues that faced children or adults in the past and write persuasive statements that persons from history might have written.)

--Writing predictions for outcomes of current events or of historical events being studied. (Confirm or revise the predictions on the basis of new information.)

--Writing biographies of historical figures studied or discussed in class. (Use several sources of information to gather the data and make a list of sources. Dress up as the persons and have classmates read the biographies to the class.)

--Brainstorming and listing careers related to social studies. (Choose careers for further study and take notes for an oral report. Write a class invitation to a person in one of these career fields, requesting a career interview. Discuss and list questions for a career interview which will help the person discuss the responsibilities of the job, his or her feelings about the job, preparation for the job, and similar topics. After the interview, evaluate interview skills both orally and in writing.)

When the writing activity is a natural outgrowth of the content being studied, learning in the content area can be reinforced at the same time that skills in written communication are strengthened.

Some writing activities should be created and structured by the teacher. Other writing activities should be initiated by the students and based on their interests. Whether writing is assigned by teachers or initiated by students, teachers should help students generate, develop, organize, refine, and share their written ideas.

A detailed curriculum guide thus provides crucial support for effective instruction in writing in the elementary school social studies classroom. Such a guide should communicate the program of study in terms of content and skills to be mastered. It also should provide much-needed sets of behaviorally stated objectives and potentially useful student learning materials. But it can do even more. A useful curriculum guide in writing can also provide teachers with examples of study aids, sample instructional strategies, suggested teaching techniques, and evaluation procedures needed to translate the program of study into specific lessons. A truly useful writing curriculum guide is much more than a simple educational program outline. Such a guide serves in effect as an inservice training guide, for these added ingredients actually show teachers how to carry out the program components. Experience indicates that such training is indispensable to a successful writing program.

Staff Development

Given the virtual absence of preservice teacher preparation for teaching writing, inservice training is almost a necessity if the ingredients of a good writing curriculum guide are to become a classroom reality. Inservice training serves many purposes in addition to developing teachers' skills and expertise. Probably its most important purpose is to help teachers internalize the concepts of a writing program and develop a sense of ownership of the program.

Effective staff-development programs in the teaching of writing can be cooperatively planned with nearby universities. If that possibility does not exist, a school district can establish its own program, drawing on both outside consultants and the talents of its best teachers of writing. Teachers working with teachers can provide an invaluable dimension to a staff-development program. Schools can also take advantage of outside help; community members who write well can share experiences with teachers, as can master writing teachers from other school districts. Inservice training may involve purely individual efforts, informal teacher-sharing efforts, and more-formal organized staff-development projects.

Teachers may initiate and design their own training in teaching writing in their social studies classes. A number of films, books, and pamphlets are valuable sources of ideas and strategies.[2] Teachers may wish to try some of the specific strategies described in this book or demonstrated in college courses or professional workshops. Working with colleagues, individual teachers can adapt these ideas for use with their own students. By observing classes where such strategies are being tried, teachers can provide helpful suggestions to one another. Moreover, by trying ideas generated by their colleagues, teachers can assist each other while at the same time adding to their own repertoires of writing instruction strategies. Through independent reading and informal classroom experimentation, teachers can develop a readiness for teaching writing in elementary school social studies. As this readiness is developed or while it is developing, schools can move toward more-formal inservice programs.

Opportunities to share ideas about writing in their classrooms provide teachers with a useful link between self-study and inservice training. No matter how unfamiliar they may be with the technicalities of writing, most teachers can contribute to such sharing efforts. Teachers may meet, for example, to share assignments that have produced successful writing. A well-constructed assignment helps students focus their ideas and produce better writing. Teachers from one school district identified 12 characteristics of a well-constructed writing assignment:

--It is meaningful or significant to the students.

--It is related to the program of studies.

--It concerns a subject about which the students have information or can locate information.

--It defines and limits the subject.

--It clearly specifies the tasks for the students.

--It encourages students to direct writing toward a specific audience.

--It encourages thinking and originality.

--It enables students to discover new understandings.

--It suggests a form (e.g., letter, script, speech, diary, dialogue) or lends itself to a variety of forms.

--It provides for differences in students' abilities.

--It enables students to understand the basis on which they are being evaluated.

--It is appropriate to the grade level of the students.

Useful guidelines for making writing assignments in social studies can also emerge from such sharing sessions. For example, in planning writing assignments teachers may want to proceed according to the following steps (with examples from a typical grades 5-6 social studies program):

Step 1. Review the body of knowledge to determine the key concepts or facts that are to be taught.

--If a unit of study, determine the generalizations that hold it together (for example, southeastern United States).

--If a portion of a unit, determine the information or skills to be learned (for example, life on a colonial plantation).

--If a generalization, determine the sections of the text that pertain to the generalization (for example, slavery).

Step 2. Identify logical writing activities that will add to students' understanding of the concept.

Step 3. Consider the purposes of the writing.

--If to motivate interest or to initiate learning, the whole class can brainstorm data so that individuals can write about the topic even if they have not studied it.

--If to determine the present knowledge of students, ask students to write about a topic prior to studying it.

--If to reinforce learning, students can write about their understandings of a given topic.

--If to generate new knowledge or develop new understandings and insights, students can be asked to write about a topic that they must research or to write about known data with a new perspective (for example, writing about a topic from the viewpoint of two different people or applying data to a new body of information).

Step 4. Use a variety of writing experiences that offer students opportunities to explore different forms, write for different audiences, and write from different points of view.

--For grade 5: business letter, social note, news report, outline, biography, commercial for radio or television, folktale, adventure or fantasy story, factual paragraph, haiku, limerick.

--For grade 6, autobiography, feature article, interview, job application, persuasive paragraph, script for a skit, legend, heroic adventure, mystery or science fiction story, personal experience, diamante, free verse.

Step 5. Increase the level of difficulty of writing assignments.

--Move from easy assignments to harder ones (for example, from descriptive and sequenced or chronological paragraphs to persuasive and analytical paragraphs).

--Move from short assignments requiring simple skills to longer assignments requiring more-complex skills.

--Move from concrete to abstract ideas.

--Move from teacher-directed tasks to student-directed tasks.

Step 6. Match content objectives with objectives naturally related to the writing activities.

Step 7. Plan appropriate activities for each phase of the writing process: prewriting, composing, revising, and sharing.

Step 8. Write the assignment yourself so that you can experience the thinking process that the students will experience and identify any problems related to the clarity of the assignment.

Step 9. Revise the assignment.

Teachers may also wish to meet to share writing activities they have read about or used. Depending on the depth of their concern and involvement, they may wish to discuss ideas about many other aspects of writing as well. These sharing sessions can be informally organized around questions expressing common concerns. A series of questions such as those that follow can form the basis for an open discussion on managing classroom time and space, evaluating student writing, and encouraging students to write.[3]

Managing Classroom Time and Space

--In what ways can language arts and social studies be integrated to allow maximum use of instructional time?

--How can the classroom be structured so as to enhance independent student writing activities?

--What cooperative student writing activities can be designed to increase the potential of peer assistance?

Evaluating Student Writing

--How should student work be evaluated?

--What are some different methods for evaluating papers?

--Should every piece of writing be revised?

--What are some productive alternatives to grading each piece of student writing?

--How often should teachers have conferences with students?

Encouraging Students to Write

--What encourages students to write?

--What inhibits writing?

--How can teachers motivate students to write?

--What are some ways to share student writing?

--How often should students write?

To ensure the most effective teaching of writing in the elementary school social studies classroom, however, teachers should go beyond sharing ideas and techniques. They should also engage in organized efforts to correlate writing with social studies learning objectives, to design sequences of writing activities that can be used in their own classes with their own texts, to develop specific exercises through which students can learn basic writing skills using social studies content, and to practice creating effective writing assignments. These efforts may well require more-formal inservice training.

Organized, systematic inservice programs come in many forms, ranging from a short one-time training session to a continuing series of sessions over a period of weeks or months. Although one-shot teacher workshops do not as a rule bring about much significant classroom change, they can sometimes serve useful purposes, especially when they stimulate teachers' interest in writing, make teachers aware of the possibilities for and need of instruction in writing in their classrooms, and introduce teachers to some useful teaching techniques. However, the kind of training that usually seems most valuable consists of continuing instruction by and feedback from teachers who are experienced in teaching writing in their own classrooms (perhaps graduates of major writing projects or of special college or university writing courses or programs) and curriculum specialists in writing and (in this case) social studies.

While such inservice efforts may take a number of forms, the most promising share the following four features:

1. In these workshops, the teachers themselves write. Although many are reluctant to do so, they should write repeatedly, not only to realize that they can write (and that they have, in fact, plenty of things to write about, as do their students) but also to try out the procedures that they will be using with students. During this process, teachers begin to develop a feeling for what writing involves for the youngsters--a sensitivity to young writers' struggles to "find something I can write about" and the problems related to correct usage, grammar, and spelling.

2. Practical techniques are introduced, practiced, and analyzed and adaptations are made.

3. Specific and varied teaching techniques are combined to form viable teaching strategies that accomplish specific objectives.

4. Such workshops not only transmit information about the curriculum and teaching, they involve the participants in actually developing procedures, materials, and lessons to use in their own classrooms.

This final point is most important. Teachers, like beginning writers, must feel a sense of ownership of a curriculum if it is to become a part of their classroom teaching. Thus, they need to engage in workshop activities in which they experience, analyze, and discuss the major stages of the writing process. They need to learn a variety of techniques that can be used in the prewriting stage to help students learn how to generate ideas, evaluate and accommodate a specific audience, and focus on topics. Teachers' study of the composing process should include strategies for helping students organize written statements and tips for making assignments that help students rather than confusing them. In working with the revision stage of writing, teachers need to focus on ways to undertake the various tasks that need to be done at this stage, including providing peer as well as teacher feedback, revising a draft, editing final drafts, and evaluating students' written work.

School principals and key teachers can provide instructional leadership in conducting staff-development programs that incorporate these features. A strong program can evolve if several principals and teachers in the same school system jointly plan a series of inservice workshops and exchange teacher talent from school to school.

Under the guidance of central-level supervisors and specialists, a large school district may plan a standard inservice workshop model in order to ensure consistency in the program. Such a workshop can be designed in advance and taught to principals or other workshop leaders in special training sessions. If they are provided with step-by-step directions, a time schedule, and prepared handouts, principals may welcome the opportunity to serve as instructional leaders.

One possible format for such an inservice program might be a series of 90-minute teacher meetings over the course of a semester, each meeting planned to deal in depth with a specific aspect of teaching writing. Each session could consist of a general introductory presentation by the workshop leader, a carefully structured large-group discussion, and a small-group activity. One such meeting, on the topic of developing effective writing assignments, might be organized according to the following pattern.[4]

Introductory Presentation (20 minutes)

1. Welcome teachers and introduce self.

2. Review workshop goals: (1) to establish good reasons for teaching writing in the social studies program, (2) to provide teachers with strategies for teaching writing through social studies, and (3) to provide teachers with concrete help in developing effective writing assignments.

3. Present a brief rationale on the importance of writing for discovering ideas, organizing information, and learning content.

Large-Group Discussion (35 minutes)

1. Discuss considerations for planning writing assignments.

2. Lead participants in brainstorming the characteristics of a well-constructed writing assignment. List ideas on chalkboard.

3. Distribute handout with list of characteristics. Ask participants to review list, add new ideas, or revise listed ideas.

4. Distribute a handout of model writing assignments in social studies. Ask participants to analyze each of these assignments.

Small-Group Task (35 minutes)

1. Organize participants into groups of three, asking them to group according to the social studies texts they are teaching.

2. Ask participants to write one or two assignments (following the model) that they can use with their students and their texts.

3. Have a recorder write the assignments on paper and hand them to workshop leader.

4. Ask the groups to share the assignments they wrote.

Followup

1. Distribute copies of all assignments made at the workshop to each teacher participant.

2. At a later session in the series, ask participants to describe their experiences with selected assignments and offer suggestions for improving them.

Such inservice activities require instructional input by experienced teacher/writers or by writing/social studies experts. They also require sharing, hard work, and creative energy on the part of teachers. However, the results are well worth the effort and cost.

Teacher/Administration Assessment

A third key to successful elementary school social studies writing instruction is a cooperative teacher/administrator assessment plan. Teachers may want to establish for themselves teaching improvement goals and jointly plan with their supervising administrators a method for evaluating their progress in meeting these teaching goals.

It is helpful to establish a list of questions that will assist the teacher and the supervising administrator in reviewing the classroom program. Such a list may include some of the following questions:

Provision for All Stages of the Writing Process

--Is there frequent writing in class?

--Is emphasis placed on the importance of generating, expanding, and focusing ideas?

--Are students taught to organize their ideas?

--Do students participate in an editing process by proofreading and revising?

--Do students share their writing?

<u>Provision for the Needs of All Students</u>

--Do assignments provide for the different abilities of students?

--Do assignments provide for the different backgrounds and interests of students?

--Are different types of writing assignments given?

<u>Evaluation of Students' Writing</u>

--Does the evaluative instrument reflect the specific elements stressed in each assignment?

--Do students have a checklist of the criteria by which their writing will be judged?

--Do students have individual folders containing compositions that reflect their growth in writing skills?

<u>Assessing the School Program</u>

--Is there both pre- and post-testing of writing skills?

--Are the results of the assessment used in determining whether objectives have been met?

--Are the results of the assessment used in preparing objectives for the following year?

--Is the suggested procedure used to assess the progress and needs of particular groups of students?

Assessment of a writing program can perhaps best be accomplished by comparing papers written at the beginning of the school year with those produced at the end of the school year. Using a general-impression or holistic approach, three teachers can quickly read both sets of papers (coded to conceal students' names and dates), ranking each paper in one of three or four categories (from very good to satisfactory to not-so-good to poor). The papers can then be decoded to determine how many students improved and how much they improved between the fall and the spring. Appropriate instructional activities for the next semester can then be planned.

Summary

And this brings us back to Alice*:

> . . .and still the Queen cried, "Faster! Faster!" and dragged her along. "Are we nearly there?," Alice managed to pant out at last.
>
> "Nearly there!" the Queen repeated. "Why, we passed it ten minutes ago! Faster!," and they ran on for a time in silence, with the wind whistling in Alice's ears, and almost blowing her hair off her head, she fancied.
>
> "Now! Now!" cried the Queen. "Faster! Faster!" And they went so fast that at last they seemed to skim through the air, hardly touching the ground with their feet, till suddenly, just as Alice was getting quite exhausted, they stopped, and she found herself sitting on the ground breathless and giddy.
>
> The Queen propped her up against a tree, and said kindly, "You may rest a little, now."
>
> Alice looked round her in great surprise. "Why, I do believe we've been under this tree the whole time! Everything's just as it was!"
>
> "Of course it is," said the Queen. "What would you have it?"
>
> "Well, in *our* country," said Alice, still panting a little, "you'd generally get to somewhere else--if you ran very fast for a long time as we've been doing."
>
> "A slow sort of country!," said the Queen. "Now, *here*, you see, it takes all the running *you* can do, to keep in the same place. If you want to get somewhere else, you must run at least twice as fast as that!"

Writing in elementary school social studies need not be a confusing wonderland. Teachers can "run" with a writing program in this content area, given the three basic supports noted here: a detailed curriculum guide, inservice staff development, and an adequate teacher/administrator assessment program--and, unlike Alice, they can get somewhere.

---

*Reprinted with permission from *Alice's Adventures in Wonderland and Through the Looking Glass*, by Lewis Carroll (New York: Collier Books, a division of Macmillan Publishing Co., Inc.; London: Collier Macmillan Publishers, 1962). Copyright 1962 by Macmillan Publishing Co., Inc.

Notes

1. From *Guide for Teaching Writing, K-6, in the Fairfax County Public Schools*, Part 1 (Fairfax, Va.: Fairfax County Public Schools, 1970).

2. See the epilogue to this book for a list of some useful sources.

3. Based on materials developed by Betty Blaisdell and Dolores Bohen, English curriculum specialist in the Fairfax County (Virginia) Public Schools.

4. From *Guide for Teaching Writing, 7-12, in the Fairfax County Public Schools* (Fairfax, Va.: Fairfax County Public Schools, 1977).

20. THREE ESSENTIALS FOR A SOUND SOCIAL STUDIES/WRITING PROGRAM

By Barry K. Beyer

Attention to the principles of good classroom teaching, as Nellie Quander explains in Chapter 18, is crucial to the success of any elementary school social studies/writing program. And, as Betty Blaisdell and I point out in the preceding chapter, an adequate curriculum guide, appropriate staff development, and continued assessment of student writing and classroom teaching provide indispensable support for the classroom implementation of such a program. Yet none of these factors--as important as they are--is as crucial to the success of a social studies/writing program as the soundness of the program itself. This article analyzes three essential features of a sound program.

Let me make clear what I mean by a "sound program." The measure of any social studies/writing program, in my judgment, is the extent to which such a program accomplishes two crucial goals: (1) student mastery of progressively more-sophisticated and mature principles of written discourse in social studies subject-matter areas and (2) student mastery of basic social studies information, concepts, generalizations, and skills. In elementary school social studies, writing should serve as a means for learning social studies as well as a goal of learning. Conversely, social studies subject matter should serve as a vehicle for learning or improving writing as well as a goal of learning. A sound social studies/writing program leads to increased learning of both writing and social studies, as determined by all measures of student achievement. These goals are not likely to be achieved unless the program is constructed in a way that deliberately fosters their achievement.

Three features distinguish a sound elementary school social studies/writing program. First, such a program must provide for sequential skill development across grade levels. Second, it must integrate skills with subject-matter instruction. And third, it must explicitly provide for direct instruction in both writing and subject matter.

The claim that an elementary school social studies/writing program should be sequential, integrative, and explicitly instructional is based on neither whim nor theory. It is based on what we know both about writing and about the present state of teacher expertise in the teaching of writing in the elementary school.

Writing is not a skill; it is a complex process that makes use of a repertoire of discrete skills. Nor is writing something that is mastered once and for all at a particular time in one's schooling and then used in unchanging fashion thereafter. Writing grows and develops over time as it is used for a variety of purposes in a variety of contexts. Nor is there only one kind of writing to be used with all types of information or for all purposes. A variety of writing forms and styles exist for use in achieving many different goals in many different content areas. No single writing style or form is appropriate for all content areas and purposes. Acknowledgment of these three major characteristics of writing must shape the teaching of writing, if we are to improve the quality of student writing and learning in our schools.

Furthermore, few elementary school teachers have had formal training in the teaching of writing. Of course, most wrote when they were themselves students. Freshman English composition was and still is an inescapable hurdle for most college students. The ever-present term paper continues to rear its ugly head in course after college course. In spite of these writing requirements, however, most preservice teachers received precious little instruction in how to compose--how to generate ideas, how to organize and relate information, and how to put words, ideas, and information together in order to accomplish a specific purpose for a specific audience. With the exception of the relatively few teachers who have had the opportunity to become involved in such efforts as the National Writing Project and other inservice writing programs, classroom teachers in general know little about how to teach writing effectively to their students.

School systems that are interested in improving the writing skills of their students must thus consider both the nature of writing and the lack of teacher expertise in writing if they are to achieve the learning goals they seek. Benign neglect will not produce the long-run improvement that NAEP test scores suggest is needed.[1] Only by developing system-wide or building-wide curricula which carefully sequence and integrate writing with subject matter and which provide for direct classroom instruction in writing can schools be assured of making improvements in the learning of both writing and social studies.

Sequential Writing Skill Development

No K-6 program of studies in any skill or subject area stands alone. Not only must it relate to programs of study in other K-6 subject-matter areas, it is also an integral part of a larger K-12 learning program. This is especially true of a writing program. To a large extent, a K-6 writing program seeks to develop the skills and knowledge necessary to achieve the skills, knowledge, and affective goals sought at the secondary and higher levels. Thus, planning a K-6 writing program involves determining what a student should be able to do by way of writing upon graduation from high school and then planning backward to identify what needs to be done at each preceding grade level to introduce, develop, and reinforce whatever is prerequisite to that goal. If educators decide that upon graduation from high school the average student should be able to write a coherent, error-free paragraph, a research report, or an analytical or persuasive essay, certain skills need to be developed in sequence at earlier grade levels in order to ensure the realization of these goals. Any K-6 program in writing needs to be developed, not as an end in itself, but as a part--a very fundamental part--of a larger K-12 sequence of learning goals and activities.

For optimum learning, skills should be introduced when appropriate to the ability levels of the students. Instruction in each grade level should build on skills introduced in earlier grades and develop foundations for skills to be introduced in later grades. Thus, for example, students may move from dictating sentences to writing a simple sentence to writing more-complex sentences. In paragraph writing, students often move from writing three-sentence paragraphs to five-sentence paragraphs and then to three-paragraph statements and so on. They may write first for entertainment or recreation, next to inform, and eventually to promote or defend.

To illustrate the sequencing of writing skill instruction, consider report writing. The report is a common writing form in social studies. Report writing as a process consists of a number of skills that can be taught in sequence as students move through the elementary school social studies curriculum. The sequence of such skill learning might begin in second grade and unfold as follows:[2]

Grade 2. The students will write about personal experiences, relating the events in chronological order.

Grade 3. The students will write short reports, successfully completing the following tasks:

--Collect and record important facts to be included.

--Organize the relevant facts in logical order.

--Share the written report with classmates.

Grade 4. The students will write short reports on given topics, successfully completing the following tasks:

--Pose two or three interesting questions about the topic.

--Find answers to the questions by gathering information from one or more sources.

--Take brief notes while reading to find information.

--Organize the facts into logical order.

--Write the report, using source notes.

--Provide a concise, interesting title.

--Prepare a brief bibliography, following a model.

Grade 5. The students will write short factual reports, successfully completing the following tasks:

--Pose questions about the topic.

--Gather information from two or more sources.

--Take brief notes to answer the questions posed and to record other important information.

--Organize information into an outline which contains topics and subtopics.

--Write the report, using the outline.

--Provide a concise, interesting title.

--Prepare a bibliography, supplying title, author, and copyright date for each entry.

Grade 6. The students will write reports and biographies, successfully completing the following tasks:

--Select a limited subject that is personally interesting.

--Research the subject, using several sources of information.

--Take brief notes, summarizing information on note cards.

--Plan the report by organizing the notes and developing an outline.

--Write and proofread a preliminary draft.

--Rewrite the report, refining style and correcting errors.

--Illustrate the report with maps, diagrams, transparencies, or other visual aids.

--Prepare a bibliography, supplying author, title, publisher, place of publication, and copyright date for each entry.

Such a sequence obviously does not stand alone but fits in carefully with similar sequential development of sentence writing, punctuation, and other skills. Furthermore, while every writing activity should attend to the three major stages of the writing process--prewriting, composing, and revising--instruction might well be on only selected aspects of each stage at each grade level. In the early grades, students should receive instruction in how to generate ideas to write about (a prewriting skill) and how to develop focus. For example, they might move from learning how to build word caches to more-formal brainstorming, using focus groups and data-gathering charts. Organizing ideas and information in paragraph form should receive attention when students are ready for it--perhaps in the early intermediate grades. Such specific skills as forecasting and sequencing should await attention until the secondary grades.

In planning an overall developmental writing program, teachers should thus consider at least six variables at each grade level: content, task, length, skill focus, subject focus, and audience. As a general rule, students in the primary grades write first about real experiences or concrete objects, events, or places (but, as Kieran Egan argues, "real" experiences may also include the products of youngsters' very vivid imaginations[3]), moving gradually to abstract representations of these things and to more-abstract ideas. In terms of tasks, they may move from writing descriptions and narratives to explaining how and why and to writing persuasive arguments. Initial writing assignments should be short, with tasks becoming longer and more complex as students evidence competence in the early writing tasks--moving gradually from phrases to sentences, combinations of sentences, simple and then complex paragraphs, short three-paragraph statements, and finally to short essays.

Young students can also attend to audience, at a simple level. In the primary grades, they may write to friends, parents, siblings, and even government officials or famous people. Research suggests, however, that systematic analysis of audience should be postponed at least until the upper-intermediate grades. Finally, what we ask students to write about may move from their own selves or other specific individuals in early elementary school, to groups of close acquaintances and groups in general in middle school, to society as a whole in high school.

Elementary school writing programs must also attend to two other major concerns, in turn: (1) creating in the students a willingness to write and (2) helping them use writing for meaningful, subject-matter-related purposes. To accomplish the first goal, a writing program must create a classroom climate that is supportive of writing. It must also recognize and utilize the dozens of opportunities for writing that exist in the normal classroom routine as well as in elementary school social studies course work. Students need opportunities to see written words, to hear them read aloud, and to see them written down and then read aloud. Young children need to see others write--especially parents, teachers, and peers. They need to write in conjunction with other media, including pictures, films, music, oral reports, and reading. They need to write even when what they write is undecipherable. Moreover, all these activities need to be conducted in a nonthreatening atmosphere of trust and support. The products of students' writing need to be shared with their peers and with adults in positive ways.

After the proper atmosphere is established, students can write in specific social studies areas for subject-matter learning purposes rather than merely for self-expression or recreation. They can write to develop plans for further learning by inventing ideas to study later. They can write from different points of view in order to develop new insights into what they are studying. And they can write to pull together ideas studied earlier. The writing skills taught or employed in such activities must be appropriate not only to the abilities of the students but also to the content being studied and the substantive goals that the writing seeks to accomplish.

Thus, a carefully sequenced writing program should move students from simple, basic skills to more-complex ones, from skill-by-skill use to conscious use of the entire writing process, and from competence in one technique to familiarity with a variety of techniques and forms. Such a program must also move students gradually from highly teacher-directed to increasingly self-directed writing. Finally, in terms of social studies, it should move students away from self-centered writing and thinking toward other-centered and socially focused concerns.

Skill and Content Integration

A sound writing program integrates the development of writing skills with other aspects of the program of studies. This integration can occur in at least four areas. In elementary school social studies, writing instruction should be combined with social studies learning objectives, with social studies content and subject matter, with other skill development--especially reading comprehension--and with a variety of other learning activities. Skill development and subject-matter learning should proceed together for motivational as well as for learning purposes.

First, writing skills objectives must be integrated with social studies learning objectives.[4] If, for instance, a major elementary school social studies objective is "to identify the roles and contributions of famous Americans," a writing skill objective that can be accomplished simultaneously might be "to expand basic sentences by adding information that tells where, when, how, what kind, and so on." An activity that seeks to achieve these two objectives simultaneously might present students with a simple sentence about a famous American and ask them to expand the sentence by adding appropriate information about that individual's roles or contributions. For example:

Given:	George Washington was the first president.
Expanded:	George Washington, a Virginian and a plantation owner, was the first president of the United States.

Many common writing and social studies objectives can be combined in similar fashion. Elementary school students are often asked to identify and explain the significance of important events in American history. Combining several short sentences to produce a single, more-complex sentence is a writing task that can be accomplished during this process, as illustrated by the following fifth-grade assignment:

> Match each item from Column A with the item in Column B that best tells its importance in American history.

	Column A		Column B
_____	1. Eli Whitney invented the cotton gin.	A.	The Louisiana Purchase more than doubled the size of the United States.
_____	2. Jamestown was a colony.	B.	The cotton gin made it possible to grow more cotton, and so more plantations sprang up using more slaves.
_____	3. The United States bought land from France in 1803.	C.	This was the first permanent English colony in the Americas.

> After you have matched these items, rewrite each pair (combine them) into one sentence. You can add or change words, but do not leave out any information.
>
> Example: Eli Whitney's invention of the cotton gin made it possible to grow more cotton, and so more plantations sprang up using more slaves.

Combining writing with social studies objectives is a crucial feature of a sound elementary school social studies curriculum if students are to develop writing skills and learn social studies in the process. Students can use writing to learn the information and ideas they are studying about. They can use writing to invent ideas about a topic which can serve as hypotheses for testing by further study. They can also write about an event from the points of view of the different people involved in order to develop empathy for these people as well as to acquire new insights about the subject. This process is illustrated by the following assignment:

> After reading the assigned pages in your text, pretend that you are a settler in Jamestown Colony who is living in a bark hut during his first winter in America. Write a short letter to your brother or sister in England, describing what your life in America is like so far. You may wish to share how you feel about what has occurred or what you hope will occur in the spring as well as tell some of the things that have happened.

In more-analytical fashion, students can write short paragraphs about a series of related topics and then, using data from their paragraphs, compare these topics and make generalizations.

1. The natural resources of the South influenced the lives of the people who lived there in colonial times.

2. The natural resources of the South influence the lives of people living there today.

3. The natural resources of the South have affected the lives of people who lived there in colonial times and Southerners today in different ways.

Writing can be used to teach basic social studies concepts as well as to clarify insights into key themes and topics. By writing specific examples of ideas or concepts, students can develop important social studies generalizations.

Writing instruction should be combined with efforts to develop other skills; for example, skimming, observing, and careful reading. Children can quickly examine one or more study prints or pictures or skim a brief reading and then write about what these items seem to "say." Later, they can study these same items in depth to see if in fact they do "say" what the students thought they said. Students can then revise their original statements, changing their conclusions if necessary or using their initial conclusions as topic sentences.

Finally, writing should be integrated with other learning media and techniques as students seek to accomplish social studies learning goals. While the writing process may serve as the structure of social studies lessons, such media as filmstrips, documents, oral reports, and texts can be used in conjunction with specific writing activities, as shown by the following learning sequence:[5]

1. Students view the filmstrip Life on a Plantation to observe what life was like for whites and blacks.

2. The class brainstorms lists (recorded on the board) of what they saw under the headings "Life of Slave Owners," "Life of Slaves," and "Plantation Activities."

3. Small groups evaluate the lists on the board to prepare two other lists: "Benefits of Slavery" and "Evils of Slavery." The small groups then report to the class.

4. The class lists (on the board) some arguments that a person opposed to slavery might have made.

5. Students pretend that they have just visited a plantation in the mid-1800s. Half the class, as individuals, write letters to friends describing life on the plantation from the point of view of someone favoring slavery.

6. Working in pro/con slavery pairs, students read each other's letters to learn the arguments used by the other side. Each student suggests one additional item to be included in the partner's revised letter.

7. The class analyzes two documents (a letter critical of slavery and a newspaper editorial defending plantation slavery) to find examples of arguments that might be used in their letters. Each student chooses one fact or argument to include in a revised letter.

8. Students revise their letters to include suggestions made in class and in the documents they analyzed.

9. Students read each other's revised letters and suggest corrections in spelling, punctuation, and sentence structure (by circling suspected errors). When letters are returned, students discuss reasons for the changes and make changes that they believe should be made.

10. After letters have been graded, they are posted. Each student reads four letters representing each side of the issues involved in the argument over slavery.

11. Working with partners, students write a paragraph that explains three issues involved in the slavery debate.

12. After a list of these issues is posted on the board, the class uses them to make three generalizations about slavery. Students then read the assigned pages in the text to assess whether their generalizations accurately summarize the major issues that led to the Civil War.

This sequence of classroom activities illustrates how writing can be integrated with other media and techniques to accomplish social studies learning goals and to develop writing skills.

Direct Skill Instruction

Making explicit provisions for direct skill instruction constitutes the third and most essential feature of a sound writing program in elementary school social studies. Children do not learn new skills simply by attempting them to the best of their abilities when they are required to do so. They learn a skill when they use the skill to accomplish a meaningful substantive goal, when they attend to how they execute the skill, and when they receive corrective feedback and instruction as they do so. Any effective writing skill program requires direct instruction in the various skills that constitute writing as youngsters deal with the subject matter of the program.

Direct instruction in writing can be provided at every phase of the writing process. Such instruction may consist of (1) using a strategy specifically designed to introduce and reinforce skills, (2) providing frequent supervised practice accomplished by immediate feedback and reinforcement, (3) providing supervised skill practice that is analogous to as well as equivalent to the form in which the skill is normally used, and (4) providing such instruction at each major stage of the writing process.

To introduce, review, or provide additional instruction about any writing skill or form, a teacher can use a five-step process in which the teacher (1) introduces the skill to be taught by label, definition, and/or example, (2) explains the specific steps involved in using the skill, and (3) demonstrates (using appropriate subject matter) the skill. The students then (4) practice the skill repeatedly with other appropriate content and (5) review after each practice how they did the skill and how they engaged in the various operations that constitute the skill. This skill-teaching strategy can be used repeatedly to provide direct instruction in any aspect of writing.

While instruction in writing should be frequent, it should not be long and drawn out. As Janet Cuenca notes in Chapter 16, it should be in "small bites"--lessons or activities requiring no more than 15 or 20 minutes. Students should receive immediate instructive and reinforcing feedback from the teacher or their peers. Instruction can be provided during any prewriting, composing, or revising activity, depending on the emphasis of the program at each grade level. For example, students can receive instruction in organizing their writing by following models as they compose--models such as those used in the poetry-writing activity described by Ann Gibson in Chapter 11. Teacher-made feedback models or

Figure 7

SELF-DIRECTED WRITING GUIDE

Topic: The Jamestown Settlement

1. List three pieces of information about this topic that you find in Chapter 1. You do not have to write them in sentences. Just write down bits and pieces of information that you find as you skim the chapter. Three sample items have been provided to help you start your list.

   --shortage of corn

   --many people died of malaria

   --fighting between Indians and Europeans

   --

   --

   --

2. Now write a sentence that summarizes the information above. Do not just copy the pieces of information you listed. Instead, put the information into different words so that the facts are connected to one another.

3. Next, write a paragraph. Use the sentence from task 2 as your topic sentence. Add sentences giving at least three pieces of information from task 1. These sentences should support or explain your topic sentence. Be sure to show how each piece of information is connected to your topic sentence.

4. Write a sentence that sums up the importance of the paragraph you wrote in task 3 (above). It should answer the question "So what?"

5. Now reread Chapter 1 carefully to answer these questions:
   a. What facts can you find to prove that your last sentence is true?

   b. What facts can you find to prove that this sentence may not be (completely) true?

   c. What three new ideas about this topic did you get by rereading this chapter?

questions written on a chalkboard may provide guidance during the revision process, as can more direct instruction following the five-step procedure outlined above.

Not all instruction need be teacher directed, however. Teachers can provide indirect assistance by preparing various types of guides for students to use as they write. The handout in Figure 7 illustrates one form that such a guide might take for use in fourth-, fifth-, or sixth-grade social studies. This guide leads students through the prewriting and composing stages of the writing process in combination with a reading activity. The students use their conclusions (item 5) as hypotheses to be tested by further reading in their texts and then again as topic sentences in revised versions of their original paragraphs. When this type of guide is used in the classroom, the teacher is free to move from student to student, providing individual instruction as needed.

Finally, instruction and practice in writing can be provided in forms analogous to but not equivalent to the way a particular skill is used in writing. In order to learn how to organize a paragraph by assembling details that support a topic sentence, it is not always necessary for students to invent appropriate sentences and details. Students can examine existing sentences to identify these parts of a paragraph and then resequence them in a more desirable order. Exercises such as the following may serve this purpose:

> Which of the following sentences best includes all the others?
>
> 1. Captain Smith forced settlers to make fish nets and to plant corn.
> 2. He also ordered people to gather oysters and pick wild berries to eat.
> 3. John Smith ruled Jamestown Colony with a firm hand.
> 4. Smith punished settlers who traded tools for Indian corn.
>
> Underline whichever of the following sentences support (prove) this idea: Captain John Smith ruled the Jamestown Colony with an iron hand.
>
> 1. John Smith ordered people to make fish nets and animal traps.

2. John Smith made people gather wild berries and collect oysters.

3. Christopher Newport and John Smith argued over how best to deal with Indians.

Similar activities can be developed to help students learn or practice the skill of writing conclusions:

> Which of the sentences below best sums up the importance of this paragraph?
>
> Captain John Smith ruled the Jamestown Colony with an iron hand. He ordered people to make fish nets and animal traps when food supplies ran short. He also made them gather wild berries and dig roots.
>
> 1. Smith punished those who sold tools to the Indians for corn.
> 2. Smith's main concern was that the colony survive.
> 3. Smith made the settlers do as he ordered.

When content used in such activities is drawn from content current to the social studies topic under study, writing instruction and subject-matter instruction reinforce each other.

It should be noted that instruction is not complete until students discuss and share how they identified topic or concluding sentences or why they sequenced other sentences as they did. Mixing such analogous activities as these with direct experience in generating, composing, and revising their own paragraphs not only introduces variety into learning but also enables students to work with the maximum possible amount of subject matter.

Finally, instruction needs to be provided at each stage in the writing process in the specific skills required to complete that stage. When students are given a writing assignment, they must be shown how to generate something worthwhile to write. Students need instruction in how to brainstorm as well as opportunities to do so, and they need instruction in the many other techniques they can use to turn a topic into a topic sentence. Children also need direct instruction in how to organize their writing, whether it be single paragraphs or three-paragraph reports. They need to be shown how to rewrite in order to clarify their ideas, how to edit for grammatical and content accuracy, and how to evaluate their own writing. Skill instruction that is provided when the skill is needed to accomplish a substantive writing assignment frequently produces better learning than does drill-and-practice skill teaching, because students have a reason to learn the skill which is directly connected to the subject matter.[6]

Summary

An effective writing program in elementary school social studies must exhibit many features. Certainly the principles of good classroom instruction must be employed. Detailed curriculum guides, appropriate inservice training, and organized assessment of classroom instruction and student achievement are necessary supports for such a program. But behind all these lies the program that is the target of instruction. For best results, this program must follow an explicit sequence for developing writing skills, must integrate skill instruction with social studies subject matter and objectives, and must provide for systematic direct instruction in writing. The development and articulation of such a program is an indispensable ingredient in any effort to improve both instruction and learning in writing and social studies in the elementary grades.

Notes

1. The National Assessment of Educational Progress indicates that fewer than 50 percent of U.S. 17-year-olds in school can write an acceptable paragraph. While slight improvements in writing performance have been recorded for students at some age levels in some areas of the country over the past decade, much remains to be done. See "Implications of NAEP Writing Results for ASCD Members," ASCD Update 23, no. 2 (March 1981), pp. 1, 6.

2. From Fairfax County Program of Studies, K-6 (Fairfax, Va.: Fairfax County Public Schools, 1978).

3. Kieran Egan, Educational Development (New York: Oxford University Press, 1979).

4. The following two examples are based on a format devised by Dolores Bohen and Thomas Ward, curriculum specialists in the Fairfax County (Virginia) Public Schools.

5. Based on a sample lesson developed by social studies curriculum specialist Buddy Wishon, Fairfax County (Virginia) Public Schools.

6. Carl Bereiter, "Elementary School: Necessity or Convenience?," Elementary School Journal, May 1973, pp. 435-446.

EPILOGUE

Clearly, we are not where many people--parents, educators, and even students--believe we ought to be in terms of either writing or social studies in our elementary schools. However, as the preceding pages indicate, some classroom teachers are using strategies that can move us in a direction favored by many. As noted in the prologue, this book seeks to stimulate and/or improve student writing and mastery of social studies in elementary schools by suggesting and illustrating practical classroom techniques for integrating instruction in writing with social studies. For educators who are interested in improving the quality of student writing and social studies education at this level, the ideas presented here may be most useful. But these ideas will remain only ideas unless they are tried repeatedly in the classroom and unless they are made an explicit part of a coherent social studies writing curriculum taught by trained teachers across all elementary grades. To do this fruitfully will require more than random, uncritical trial of these techniques; it will require thoughtful curriculum development and classroom teaching. It also requires further study of the theory, research, and learning principles which undergird these practices.

To assist educators in conducting such a study, we have listed some sources that seem to us to be readable, informative, and immediately useful. Study, analysis, and discussion of the ideas and information contained in these sources will provide a useful context for the techniques described in this book. Moreover, such a study can also lead to the development of additional useful teaching techniques for improving writing in elementary school social studies and to the construction and implementation of curricula designed to achieve this goal. Once we have done this, we can integrate writing and social studies subject matter so that each plays a functional role in learning the other as well as serving a goal in itself. Accomplishing this goal is the challenge before us today.

RELATED RESOURCES IN THE ERIC SYSTEM

The resources described in this section have been entered into the ERIC (Educational Resources Information Center) system. Each is identified by a six-digit number and two letters: "EJ" for journal articles, "ED" for other documents. Abstracts of and descriptive information about all ERIC documents are published in two cumulative indexes: Resources in Education (RIE) for ED documents and the Cumulative Index to Journals in Education (CIJE) for EJ listings. This information is also accessible through three major on-line computer searching systems: DIALOG, ORBIT, and BRS.

Most, but not all, ED documents are available for viewing in microfiche (MF) at libraries that subscribe to the ERIC collection. Microfiche copies of these documents can also be purchased from ERIC Document Reproduction Service (EDRS), P.O. Box 190, Arlington, VA 22210. Paper copies (PC) of some ED documents may also be purchased from EDRS. Information about the availability of every ED document listed is included at the beginning of the abstract, along with prices for both microfiche and paper copies. If a document is not available from EDRS, the source and price are provided.

Journal articles are not available in microfiche. If your local library does not have the relevant issue of a journal, you may write for one or more reprints to University Microfilms, 300 N. Zeeb Rd., Ann Arbor, MI 48106. The following information is needed: title of the periodical or journal, title of article, name(s) of author(s), date of issue, volume number, issue number, and page numbers. All orders must be accompanied by payment in full, plus postage. Contact University Microfilms for current price information.

Beyer, Barry K. "Pre-writing and Rewriting to Learn." Social Education 43, no. 3 (March 1979), pp. 187-89. EJ 198 671.

This article describes prewriting and postwriting activities designed to aid students in submitting a polished social studies paper rather than merely a first draft. Data analysis, questioning strategies, games, simulations, and values education strategies provide sources for focusing on the topic. Rewriting involves evaluation, revision, and editing.

Beyer, Barry K. "Teaching Basics in Social Studies." _Social Education_ 41, no. 2 (February 1977), pp. 96-104. EJ 152 384.

Beyer addresses the question of which basics to teach in the social studies and how to find time to teach basics as well as everything else required in the curriculum. He gives practical hints on ways to integrate basics into conventional social studies objectives.

Beyer, Barry K., and Anita Brostoff. "The Time It Takes: Managing/Evaluating Writing and Social Studies." _Social Education_ 43, no. 3 (March 1979), pp. 194-97. EJ 198 673.

The authors suggest methods to help social studies teachers integrate writing into courses along with and in place of verbal activities. They also suggest ways to decrease time spent in the evaluation of student writing. One method is to focus on a few primary features of writing as they are defined in the goals of the assignments.

Brostoff, Anita. "Good Assignments Lead to Good Writing." _Social Education_ 43, no. 3 (March 1979), pp. 184-86. EJ 198 670.

Brostoff describes principles which achieve good writing assignments in the social studies: (1) define the content and skills teachers want students to learn, (2) devise assignments in which level of difficulty of task fits the level of the goal, (3) let students speculate on the topic, and (4) present the topic so that students know how and what to do.

Diamond, Irene M., Nancy S. Haugen, and John M. Kean, eds. _A Guide to Helping the Gifted Student Write_. Madison: Wisconsin Writing Project, 1980. 51 pp. ED 193 657. EDRS price: MF $0.91, PC $5.30; plus postage.

This booklet on teaching composition to gifted students in kindergarten through grade 12 begins by defining the term "gifted student" and stressing the importance of a good writing curriculum to those students. It then discusses (1) guidelines for creating a writing program for gifted students, (2) Benjamin Bloom's taxonomy applied to the writing process, (3) assessing growth in the gifted student's writing, (4) purposes for writing expressive, referential, literary, and persuasive forms, and (5) essay writing for gifted and talented students. An annotated bibliography lists extensive resources for teachers of gifted students.

Diamond, Irene M., Nancy S. Haugen, and John M. Kean, eds. _A Guide to Helping the Reluctant Writer_. Madison: Wisconsin Writing Project, 1980. 98 pp. ED 193 654. EDRS price: MF $0.91, PC $6.95; plus postage.

This guide examines the characteristics of the reluctant writer and suggests strategies for teachers to use when dealing with these characteristics. It also reviews the writing process, categorizes the reluctant writer according to grade level, and provides appropriate writing activities for each level. Each activity contains (1) a statement of its objective, (2) a list of materials needed, (3) the procedure to be followed, and (4) additional suggestions for using the activity.

Diamond, Irene M., Nancy S. Haugen, and John M. Kean, eds. A Guide to Tailoring Writing Assignments for the Mainstreamed Student. Madison: Wisconsin Writing Project, 1980. 87 pp. ED 193 658. EDRS price: MF $0.91, PC $6.95; plus postage.

This booklet offers teachers of mainstreamed educationally disadvantaged and learning-disabled students some practical strategies for tailoring general writing assignments to meet individual needs. The concept of mainstreaming is discussed in part 1, and general strategies for composition teachers are listed in part 2. Part 3 describes 13 specific writing assignments that feature extensive prewriting activities for the elementary/middle grades, ordered from easy to difficult, and a nine-week expository writing course for high school students. The last section suggests using writing to improve students' coping skills and presents three case studies to support that use.

Economics Can Be Elementary: 30 Jumbo Activity Cards for Teaching Reading/Writing Skills Through Economics. Bloomfield Hills, Mich.: Sandra Schurr Publications, 1978. 32 pp. ED 152 602. EDRS price: MF $0.91; plus postage. Paper copy not available from EDRS; order from Sandra Schurr Publications, 2800 N. Woodward Ave., Bloomfield Hills, MI 48013 ($4.95; $4.50 for 10 or more sets).

These activity cards present supplementary ideas and resources related to economic education for use by classroom teachers in grades K-8. The main purpose of the cards is to encourage student discovery of basic economic and consumer concepts through activities which stress reading and writing skills. Students create bulletin boards and dioramas, summarize ideas related to the topics, draw charts and graphs, take field trips to community stores and markets, define and illustrate terms on flash cards, simulate consumer roles, and write product reviews.

Fader, Daniel, et al. The New Hooked on Books. New York: Berkley, 1976. 294 pp. ED 139 021. Not available from EDRS; order from Berkley Publishing Corp., 200 Madison Ave., New York, NY 10016 ($1.75).

This anniversary edition of "Hooked on Books" adds new materials about the general educational context necessary for the success of the approach described in earlier editions. Discussions center on the difficulties of reading instruction, caused by the decreasing importance of reading in a television era; growth in the importance of peer teaching as class size increases; approaches to the teaching of writing; the need for teachers to develop a greater sense of professionalism; and practical guides to using and administering the program in elementary and secondary schools.

Ferro, Judy. "Balance Content and Skills in the Social Studies." Social Studies 71, no. 3 (May/June 1980), pp. 118-120. EJ 226 491.

The author suggests that the teaching of skills should be a major goal of all social studies courses and presents a list of activities which help to develop such skills as gathering and sharing information.

Giroux, Henry A. "Teaching Content and Thinking Through Writing." Social Education 43, no. 3 (March 1979), pp. 190-93. EJ 198 672.

This article outlines a procedure for teaching writing which helps students learn the content and thinking skills necessary for the reasoning and learning tasks required in the social studies. Sample lessons in a secondary American history course involve students in discussing, reading, problem solving, and synthesizing information.

Giroux, Henry A. "Writing and Critical Thinking in the Social Studies." Curriculum Inquiry 8, no. 4 (Winter 1978), pp. 291-310. EJ 199 416.

Giroux examines traditional theoretical assumptions about the pedagogy of writing and critical thinking and shows that they are linked dialectically. He illustrates how a pedagogy of writing can be used as a learning vehicle to help students learn and think critically about any given social studies subject.

Goolsby, Thomas M., Jr., and Joseph P. Stoltman. "Some Writing Experiences of Third Grade Students in Social Science and Reading." 1971. 83 pp. ED 058 278. EDRS price: MF $0.91, PC $6.95; plus postage.

Three sets of instructional materials were prepared by third-graders after working with and responding to similar experimental materials in reading and social science. The curriculum begins at a point when most children are able to read; however, supplementary listening passages and other readiness training and assessment are provided for those who cannot. The material generally consists of short passages followed by multiple-choice questions.

Gregory, Emily, and Mary J. Tingle, eds. Foundations for a Curriculum in Written Composition, K-6. Athens, Ga.: English Curriculum Study Center, University of Georgia, 1967. 250 pp. ED 026 364. EDRS price: MF $0.91, PC $16.85; plus postage.

Background information on the composition curriculum prepared by the English Curriculum Study Center at the University of Georgia is given in this book. Specific subjects covered include the theoretical basis, objectives, and structure of the curriculum in written composition for grades K-6; the contributions of anthropology, sociology, and psychology to the understanding of language; the structure of English; and the process of composing.

Haley-James, Shirley M., ed. Perspectives on Writing in Grades 1-8. Urbana, Ill.: National Council of Teachers of English, 1981. 131 pp. ED 198 565. EDRS price: MF $0.91, PC $10.25; plus postage. Also available from NCTE, 1111 Kenyon Rd., Urbana, IL 61801 ($5.00 member, $5.50 nonmember).

Summarizing the best current thinking about what classroom approaches produce sound writing experiences in the first eight grades, this book offers teachers a means of checking on their own practices and perceptions about how writing can best be learned. The first chapter of the book presents a historical review of authoritative opinion regarding appropriate instruction in written composition. The recommendations of those authorities are distilled into 11 observations about effective writing intruction, and these observations, in turn, provide the philosophical framework for the remaining chapters. Chapter 2 cites data gleaned in a random survey of teaching practices in use in fourth-grade classrooms, and suggests that while some of the teaching practices utilized are in concert with those recommended by the authorities cited in chapter 1, other practices are in direct conflict with a substantial body of professional literature. Reports of other successful classroom teaching practices and writing programs are detailed in chapters 3 through 6. These chapters discuss the importance of a specific purpose and audience for a piece of writing as well as the necessity of prewriting, rewriting, and evaluating writing. Chapter 7 details the trends of writing-related research in the past 50 years, the role of the classroom teacher in such research, more-recent developments in research practices, and future research needs, emphasizing the necessity of conducting writing research in context.

Howard, Deborah Fox, et al. "Writing Local History: A New Look at Old Portsmouth." Childhood Education 56, no 5 (April/May 1980), pp. 264-67. EJ 226 130.

The author presents a learning activity for involving 9- to 11-year-old children in history writing. Children toured Portsmouth, New Hampshire, interviewed residents, inspected historical documents and artifacts, kept field notes, and wrote a final narrative. Applicability to other sites is favorably assessed. Reference materials for a case study of Portsmouth are supplied.

Integration of Content and Problem Solving Skills. Schenectady: Niskayuna Central School District 1, 1979. 11 pp. ED 179 479. EDRS price: MF $0.91; plus postage. Paper copy not available.

This brief guide is designed to help teachers learn how to integrate content and problem-solving skills in the social studies curriculum. Problem-solving skills include analyzing an in-depth question/problem, selecting a format for recording information, gathering and recording information, and writing a summary. Materials in the guide include a chart showing the basic problem-solving skills process and associated subskills, an overview of one unit showing questions/problems, a sample student guide sheet showing integration of content and skills, and a sample teacher guide sheet showing answers expected from students. Eleven question/problems used to organize a unit on the American Revolution are presented. A student guide for one question provides detailed directions for problem solving. Students analyze the question through labeling nouns, verbs, and limiters, defining unfamiliar words, and restating the question. An organized form is devised by writing implied and subquestions of the larger question. A list of resources for gathering information and an outline for writing the factual summary are provided.

Klasky, Charles. "The History Mystery." Social Studies 70, no. 1 (January/February 1979), pp. 41-43. EJ 197 113.

This article describes a method for making the study of history more interesting. Based on student research and composition, the method involves students in writing both true and false "autobiographies" of famous people. Students then exchange autobiographies and determine which accounts are true and which are false.

Kroen, William C., Jr. "The Here and Now." Teacher 96, no. 5 (January 1979), pp. 82-84, 86-87. EJ 205 801.

Activities are described for developing students' interest in current events through teaching about the news media, introducing major newspapers and magazines, encouraging analysis and forecasting on current issues, and teaching news reporting, interviewing, and writing techniques, culminating in a mock presidential press conference.

Murrow, Casey, ed. *Using Our Communities: An Outline for Action in Vermont Schools*. Montpelier: Vermont Department of Education, 1977. 64 pp. ED 174 371. EDRS price: MF $0.91, PC $5.30; plus postage.

Outstanding community-based work now going on in Vermont schools is described in this booklet, which also suggests ways to develop similar work in other communities. The term "community studies" is used to encompass a broad range of activities carried out with the local community as the focus of and location for students' work. The booklet discusses ways of obtaining program support from school administrators, parents, and the local community; outlines the wide variety of experiences possible in community-based studies; and gives guidelines for planning successful field trips. The section titled "Community Studies Activities" describes 50 projects undertaken in Vermont schools which succeeded in the eyes of the teachers and children involved. Final chapters cover student writing (often the most striking success of community-oriented work), record keeping, and local and regional resources.

Page, Dorothy H. "Yankee Doodle Noodle Co. Needs You." *Teacher* 95, no. 6 (February 1978), pp. 82-93. EJ 182 636.

The author describes an activity-centered approach for an elementary language-arts project with a careers theme. It begins with exercises in which students identify different kinds of jobs and discuss and practice techniques of interviewing and culminates in the study of a specific job area--advertising. All activities emphasize the importance of subject-area skills basic to most careers.

Parker, Robert P., Jr. "From Sputnik to Dartmouth: Trends in the Teaching of Composition." *English Journal* 68, no. 6 (September 1979), pp. 32-37. EJ 209 276.

This article reviews trends in the teaching of grammar and composition and the impact of the Dartmouth Conference and the "new English" on the teaching of composition.

People, Parties and Politics: 35 Jumbo Activity Cards for Teaching Reading/Writing Skills in Social Studies. Bloomfield Hills, Mich.: Sandra Schurr Publications, n.d. 38 pp. ED 152 603. EDRS price: MF $0.91; plus postage. Paper copy not available from EDRS; order from Sandra Schurr Publications, 2800 N. Woodward Ave., Bloomfield Hills, MI 48013 ($4.95; $4.50 for 10 or more sets).

These 35 supplementary activities on American politics are designed to be used by social studies classroom teachers in elementary and junior high schools. Topics include voting, elections, presidential qualifications, presidential activities, congressional duties, political participation, terms of office, political terminology, candidates and issues, party affiliation, and political heroes. Students are involved in a variety of activities, many of which stress reading and writing skills. Activities include creating bulletin-board and scrapbook displays of newspaper articles, drawing voter timelines, inventing games around political themes, writing letters to congressmen and political party headquarters, composing essays, summarizing information gained from classroom speakers, making flash cards which define political terms, describing the background of various presidents, and writing research papers. For each activity, information is given on the background of the topic, materials and procedures, and additional learning activities.

Roselle, Daniel. "Ten Basic Suggestions to Social Studies Students for Improving Your Writing." Social Education 41, no. 2 (February 1977), pp. 113-19. EJ 152 387.

This article presents ten guidelines to help students improve their writing: clear expression, specificity, originality, avoiding stereotyping, linking paragraphs, setting time by parallel events, linking past and present, using primary sources, giving evidence for generalizations, and reading to increase sensitivity.

Scardamalia, Marlene, et al. Writing for Results: A Sourcebook of Consequential Composing Activities. Toronto: Ontario Institute for Studies in Education, 1981. 166 pp. ED 198 566. Not available from EDRS; order from OISE, 252 Bloor St. W., Toronto, Ont. M5S 1V6, Canada ($10.50).

Sixty consequential writing tasks are described in this sourcebook to help elementary and secondary school students develop their abilities in written composition. The activities foster thinking by posing game-like writing problems that require students to use their minds in the ways that good writers do, and to solve the problems that good writers manage to solve. Features of this sourcebook include a table of contents that organizes the activities according to genre, topic development, coherence, style, evaluation, and revision. An applications index cross-references activities according to a greater variety of language-arts curriculum objectives, including spelling, grammar, reading aloud, proofreading, paraphrasing, and writing topic sentences. Activities are also cross-referenced for subject-matter fields to which they can be applied, such as art, second languages, geography, and history. Detailed directions for each activity include its aim, the organization, procedure, consequences and feedback, examples, variations, and applications.

Smelstor, Marjorie, ed. A Guide to Evaluating Students' Writing. Madison: Wisconsin Writing Project, University of Wisconsin, 1978. 47 pp. ED 176 275. EDRS price: MF $0.91, PC $3.65; plus postage.

One of a series of guides to the teaching of writing at the elementary and secondary levels, this publication describes methods used in the evaluation of students' writing. Two brief introductory sections present quotations from educators which stress the value of positive evaluative comments. The third section describes procedures, advantages, and disadvantages of 11 major evaluation methods: traditional evaluation using correction symbols and letter grades, evaluation of mechanics and form, measurement of intellectual processes in writing, teacher/student conferences, peer evaluation, self-evaluation, holistic evaluation, all-staff grading, public evaluation (by an audience beyond the classroom), T-unit evaluation, and computer analysis. A fourth section describes three types of holistic evaluation scales--an analytic scale, a dichotomous scale, and a scale for assessing personal narrative writing--and presents a chart for recording mechanical errors, a composition rating scale, questions to consider in evaluating writing, and a grading guide. The final section suggests evaluation time savers, methods for creative correcting, and various evaluation gimmicks. The publication includes a list of resources for teachers.

Smelstor, Marjorie, ed. A Guide to Teaching the Importance of Audience and Subject. Madison: Wisconsin Writing Project, University of Wisconsin, 1978. 29 pp. ED 176 273. EDRS price: MF $0.91, PC $3.65; plus postage.

This publication focuses on teaching the importance of audience and subject. An introductory statement on the need to make students aware of the audience for whom they are writing is followed by a brief overview of the research concerning audience/subject relationships and lists of pertinent student needs and instructional goals. Nine suggested learning activities are then outlined; the activities are designed to instruct students in such areas as identifying purposes for writing, identifying types of audiences, and constructing messages for given audiences. Lists of resources for teachers, of possible writing forms and audiences, and of magazines that publish children's writing are also provided.

Smelstor, Marjorie, ed. A Guide to Teaching the Writing Process From Pre-Writing to Editing. Madison: Wisconsin Writing Project, University of Wisconsin, 1978. 45 pp. ED 176 274. EDRS price: MF $0.91, PC $3.65; plus postage.

This guide suggests activities to use in teaching the three stages of the composition process: prewriting, writing, and postwriting. The first four sections discuss the steps involved in the three stages of composition, research findings on the composing process, and pertinent student needs and instructional goals. The fifth section describes learning activities for the prewriting stage (including activities for motivation, listening, observation, and gathering and organizing materials), for the writing or composing stage, and for editing and proofreading. The final section suggests specific writing activities for use in the content areas of science, social studies, mathematics, English, fine arts, home economics, and business. The publication concludes with lists of suggested teacher resources.

Smelstor, Marjorie, ed. A Guide to Using Models to Teach Writing. Madison: Wisconsin Writing Project, University of Wisconsin, 1978. 87 pp. ED 176 272. EDRS price: MF $0.91, PC $6.95; plus postage.

This publication focuses on teaching writing through models that introduce ideas, patterns, and styles through specific examples. The major portion of the publication describes learning activities, grouped into seven categories according to purpose: stimulating interest for writing; developing standards for writing; showing the relationships among writer, subject, and audience; showing main ideas and supportive evidence; showing idea order and connection; showing how precise observation leads to clear, concise wording; and showing how to draw conclusions and make judgments. Within each category, activities are further subdivided according to four age levels: kindergarten through grade 3, grades 4 through 6, middle school, and high school. Other sections of the publication suggest writing models for content areas other than English, present a brief overview of research on using models to teach writing, and provide lists of sources of activities for different grade levels, stories for young children that teach mathematical concepts, "repeater" books in which sentence patterns are repeated, and recommended readings to aid in the understanding of models.

Van Nostrand, A.D. "The Inference Contract: A Model of the Writing Process." ADE Bulletin 57 (May 1978), pp. 13-20. EJ 177 586.

This article presents a taxonomy of writing instruction, a model or paradigm of the writing process, an application of this model to the teaching of writing, and an explanation of the empirical basis of the model.

Van Nostrand, A.D. "Writing and the Generation of Knowledge." Social Education 43, no. 3 (March 1979), pp. 178-180. EJ 198 668.

The author contends that students gain knowledge through the act of writing as they join bits of information into a whole. This article presents a model for scanning students' written material to determine the way ideas are related.

Ventre, Raymond. "Developmental Writing: Social Studies Assignments." Social Education 43, no. 3 (March 1979), pp. 181-183. EJ 198 669.

This article presents guidelines for social studies teachers and a sample writing assignment to encourage students' developmental writing. The author suggests that students emphasize the significance of ideas and information rather than the information itself. He establishes the relationship between thinking processes and writing and the need to break these processes into manageable steps for students.

CONTRIBUTORS

Barry K. Beyer, a professor of education at George Mason University in Fairfax, Virginia, is a specialist in social studies curriculum development and in writing. He has assisted schools throughout the nation in developing social studies and skills programs. His most recent book is Teaching Thinking in Social Studies (Columbus, Ohio: Charles E. Merrill, 1979).

Betty Jefferson Blaisdell is the English curriculum specialist for the Fairfax County (Virginia) Public Schools. Planning cooperatively with George Mason University, in 1977 she initiated the Northern Virginia Writing Project, an extension of the National Writing Project.

Beverly Chadburn has taught at every grade level in the Springfield (Oregon) school district since joining that district as a high school English teacher in 1958. Currently a media specialist, she was a member of the Oregon Writer's Project at the University of Oregon in 1980 and is active in presenting writing workshops based on Sabol and OWP methods.

Bernice Crane has taught in the Georgia elementary schools for twenty-one years and has served as instructional coordinator for the Hall County School System for three years. She was a member of the Georgia Mountain Writing Project at North Georgia College in 1979.

Janet Cuenca teaches social studies and language arts in grades 7 and 8 in the Parkway School District, St. Louis County, Missouri. She has also taught grade 6. Cuenca was recently involved in a project whose goal was to develop composition and other materials in social studies for local elementary schools.

Betty Dyarmett is a fifth-grade teacher at Fair Street Elementary School in Gainesville, Georgia. She was a 1978 participant in the Georgia Mountain Writing Project.

Susan Florio is a teacher and researcher at Michigan State University. She has taught middle-school language arts and social studies.

Joyce Howard Frank teaches second grade in the Haslett (Michigan) Public Schools. She has contributed to several books and textbooks on economics and has written numerous articles on economics education.

Ann Gibson, a fourth-grade teacher in the DeForest Area Schools in Windsor, Wisconsin, has been teaching in Ohio and Wisconsin for 15 years. She was a member of the Wisconsin Writing Project at University of Wisconsin--Madison in 1980.

Robert Gilstrap is a professor of education at George Mason University, where he teaches social studies and language arts methods. He is currently associate director of the Northern Virginia Writing Project and president of the Association for Childhood Education International.

His most recent book is Reading: A Guide for Parents (New York: John Wiley, 1982).

Wendy Giordano is a first-grade teacher at Green Acres Elementary School in Fairfax, Virginia. She was a member of the Northern Virginia Writing Project at George Mason University in 1978.

Joanne Golden is an assistant professor of education at the University of Delaware, where she teaches courses in language arts and children's literature. She is currently engaged in research on the development of writing in young children.

Ada Marie Hooper has taught primary grades for 16 years and currently teaches kindergarten at Lincoln Elementary School in Wichita, Kansas. She is a member of the Kansas Writing Project and the New Jersey Writing Project.

Dorothy Lamb is a seventh-grade remedial reading teacher at South Hall Junior High School in Gainesville, Georgia.

Jackie Martin has taught kindergarten through grade 6 in the Georgia public schools for 13 years. Her most recent teaching assignment has been at the Flowery Branch (Georgia) Elementary School.

Mary McFarland is instructional coordinator of K-12 social studies for the Parkway School District in St. Louis County, Missouri. She is the director of a federally funded project which is developing materials for teaching writing and other skills in elementary social studies.

Barbara Brody Meyer, a member of the Northern Virginia Writing Project, conducts teacher inservice training for the Fairfax County (Virginia) Public Schools. Before assuming her present position as a resource teacher, she taught grades 1 through 4.

Carol Palay has team-taught English and social studies in an 11th-grade American Civilization class at Lake Braddock Secondary School in Fairfax County, Virginia for six years. She is also a teacher consultant in the Northern Virginia Writing Project.

Virginia Pfotenhauer is a fifth-grade teacher in the Middleton-Cross Plains (Wisconsin) school system. She was a member of the Wisconsin Writing Project in the summer of 1979.

Nellie Quander was an elementary school teacher for 12 years and an elementary school principal for 13 years. She now serves as special assistant to the deputy superintendent of the Fairfax County (Virginia) Public Schools. During the 1978-1979 school year she was president of the National Association of Elementary School Principals.

Ellen Lazare Shatz is a fourth-grade teacher in P.S. 41 in the Bronx, New York. She has been teaching in elementary schools in the Bronx since 1956. Shatz is a member of the New York City Writing Project.

Kristin Smyka is the primary teacher in the elementary school in Pelican, Alaska. She is on leave of absence from Missoula (Montana) School District #1, where she taught first and second grade for five years. She was a participant in the 1980 Montana Writing Project at the University of Montana.

Carol Vukelich has been teaching in the College of Education at the University of Delaware since 1972. Currently she is investigating the writing skills of young children.

James Willcock is a fifth-grade teacher at London Towne Elementary School in Fairfax County, Virginia. He is a member of the Northern Virginia Writing Project at George Mason University.